GCSE ENGLIS-- --SH LITERATURE

Student's Book

WITHDRAWN

GEOFF BARTON

SERIES EDITOR
PETER BUCKROYD

OXFORD
UNIVERSITY PRESS

OXFORD
UNIVERSITY PRESS

Great Clarendon Street, Oxford OX2 6DP

Oxford University Press is a department of the University of Oxford.
It furthers the University's objective of excellence in research,
scholarship, and education by publishing worldwide in

Oxford New York

Auckland Bangkok Buenos Aires Cape Town Chennai
Dar es Salaam Delhi Hong Kong Istanbul Karachi Kolkata
Kuala Lumpur Madrid Melbourne Mexico City Mumbai Nairobi
São Paulo Shanghai Taipei Tokyo Toronto

Oxford is a registered trade mark of Oxford University Press
in the UK and in certain other countries

© Geoff Barton 2002

British Library Cataloguing in Publication Data

Data available

ISBN 0 19 831888 X

10 9 8 7 6 5 4 3

Printed in Italy by Rotolito Lombarda

Acknowledgments

The Publisher would like to thank the following for permission to repro-
duce photographs:

BBC Picture Library: pp 10 (left), 109 (bottom); Bury Free Press/Angela
Sharpe: p 23; Corbis/Paul Almasy: p 61 (middle); Corbis/Bettmann: pp 4,
61 (left); Corbis/Eye Ubiquitous/Chris Bland: p 113 (right); Corbis/E O
Hopper: p 6 (left); Corbis/Hulton-Deutsch Collection: p 5; Corbis/Military
Picture Library/Robin Adshead: p 38; Corbis/Papilio/Alastair Shay: p 51;
Corbis/Rothstein: p 46 (bottom left and right); Corbis/Michael Yamashita:
p 86; Corbis/Stockmarket: p 20 (top); Corel Professional Photos: pp 10
(right), 11, 90, 113 (background); Foodpix/Burke/Triolo Productions: p 109
(top); Hulton Getty: pp 46 (top), 61 (right), 72; Idols: pp 101 (left), 102; The
Illustrated London News: p 104; The Image Bank: p 82 (top left); The
Image Bank/Stuart Westmorland: p 17; Peter Jolly: p 21 (bottom right);
Keith Jones: p23; Oxford University Press: p 82 (bottom); Photodisc: pp 33,
82 (top right); The Press Association: pp 83, 101 (right); Rex Features: 14;
StockScotland/David Robertson: pp 19, 20 (bottom); Stone/Peter Cade: p 6
(right); Stone/Holly Harris: p 81 (top); Telegraph Colour Library/Candice
Farmer: p 28 (bottom); Telegraph Colour Library/Peter Gridley: p 28 (top);
Telegraph Colour Library/Tom Mackie: p 28 (middle).

Front Cover: Digital Vision (background); Corbis/Robert Estall (top); Corel
Professional Photos (second from top), Cyberzone (bottom); Oxford
University Press (second from bottom).

Artwork: Icons are by Willi Ryan. Map (page 46) Oxford University Press
Cartography Department. Map (page 66) Stefan Chabluk.

CONTENTS

ACKNOWLEDGEMENTS

Parliamentary copyright material from Statement of Health Policy by the Prime Minister delivered in the House of Commons, 22 March 2000 is reproduced with the permission of the Controller of Her Majesty's Stationery Office on behalf of Parliament.

Sample AQA (NEAB) examination questions are reproduced by permission of the Assessment and Qualifications Alliance.

We are also grateful for permission from the following to include copyright material:

James Albert, Florida Museum of Natural History for extract from research report on tropical fish.

BBC for extracts from article by Giles Turnbull: 'Get "Bloggin"', *BBC Webwise*, 5.2.02 on www.bbc.co.uk/webwise.

BBC Worldwide Ltd for recipe for 'Chocolate Brownies' from *Blue Peter Book 30*, 2000, copyright BBC Worldwide Ltd 2000.

BBC Worldwide Ltd and **Deborah Owen Literary Agency** for 'American Brownies' recipe from *Delia Smith's Complete Cookery Course* (revised 3e, BBC Worldwide, 1998), copyright © Delia Smith 1978.

Bury Free Press, Anglia Newspapers Ltd for article by Joanne Green: 'Firemen free bathroom tot' published in the *Bury Citizen*, 19.8.98.

Copyline Scotland for article by David Fickling: 'Inches from tragedy' published in *Metro*, 23.1.01.

Independent Newspapers (UK) Ltd for extract from article by Marina Baker: 'Television worthy of our times' published in *The Independent*, 5.2.02; extracts from article by David Lister: 'Kylie Minogue: Goddess of the Moment' published in *The Independent*, 23.2.02; and extracts from article by Fergal Keane: 'Tis the season to be as merry as possible' published in *The Independent*, 1.12.01.

Metro UK for graphics with article 'Inches from tragedy', *Metro*, 23.1.01.

Pentax (UK) Ltd for extract from booklet by Steven Bavister 'Take Better Photos! Hints and tips for taking better pictures with your Pentax compact camera', text copyright © Pentax (UK) Ltd, 1995, photos by Steven Bavister.

Plain English Campaign Ltd for letter-writing guide and logo, copyright © Plain English Campaign.

Practical Fishkeeping Magazine for extract from article 'Ready Steady Grow'.

Sainsbury's Supermarkets Ltd for extract from 'Citrus Fruit' leaflet.

Sutton Publishing Ltd for Death Row letter by Wallace Thomas and Jesse Morrison from *Welcome to Hell* by Jan Arriens (Ian Faulkner, Cambridge, 1991).

School of Aquatic and Fishery Sciences, University of Washington for extracts from 'Fun Fish Facts' on www.fish.washington.edu/sic/kids/fun_fish_facts.html

Transworld Publishers, a division of The Random House Group for extract from Joanne Harris: *Chocolat* (Doubleday, 1999).

Short extracts used on the following pages are also taken from copyright works:

Unit 1

pp 4–5 Texts A & D: from the diary of Kitty Kenyon cited in Lyn Macdonald: *The Roses of No Man's Land* (Michael Joseph, 1980).
pp 4–5 Texts B & E: from a letter by G. Crompton cited in *Journal of the Society of Army Historical Research*
p 5 Text C: from the autobiography of William Gibney: *Eighty Years Ago: or The Recollections of an Old Army Doctor* (Bellairs & Co, 1896).
p 6 Text A: from *A Backward Glance* by Edith Wharton (Charles Scribner's Sons, 1934)
p 6 Text B: *The Suburban Child* by James Kenward: (Cambridge University Press, 1955)

Unit 2

p 14 Text A: from *Hello!* Magazine, 2.3.02.
p 15 Text B: from *'Bullfighting: Ban the Business'*, RSPCA campaign leaflet.
p 15 Text C: from 'DNA test on dodo remains' in *Daily Mirror*, 2.3.02

Unit 3

Extracts from *Lord of the Flies* by William Golding (Faber & Faber, 1954)

Unit 4 and Examination Practice

Extracts from *Of Mice and Men* by John Steinbeck (Wm Heinemann, 1937)

Unit 5

Extracts from *The Catcher in the Rye* by J. D. Salinger (Little, Brown & Company, 1951)
p 74 Text A: from *Playback* by Raymond Chandler (Hamish Hamilton, 1958).
p 74 Text B: from *Raise the Roof Beam, Carpenters* by J. D. Salinger (Little, Brown & Company, 1963)
p 74 Text C: from *The Adventures of Huckleberry Finn* by Mark Twain (Penguin, 1966)

Unit 7

p 105 Text B: *Dickens* by Peter Ackroyd (Sinclair Stevenson, 1990)
p 111 Text A: from *Simply Spanish Islands*, Simply Travel Ltd
p 111 Text B: from 'Like driving around in an armchair' by Giles Smith, *The Guardian*, 2.10.01
p 111 Text C: from *The Locust Farm* by Jeremy Dronfield (Headline, 1998)
p 111 Text D: from 'London Docks Bombed, 1940' by Desmond Flower in Desmond Flower and James Reeves (eds): *The War 1939-1945* (Cassell, 1960).

Quick Activities for English

p 119 Extract from *A Backward Glance* by Edith Wharton (Charles Scribner's Sons, 1934)
p 120 Extract from *Spices, Salt and Aromatics in the English Kitchen* by Elizabeth David (Penguin, 1970).
p 120 Extract from *All Played Out: The Full Story of Italia '90* by Pete Davies (Heinemann, 1990)
p 121 Extract from *Speak to the Earth: Wanderings and Reflections Among Elephants and Mountains* by Vivienne de Watteville (Methuen, 1940)
p 121 Extract from *The Life of Charles Dickens* by John Forster (Hazell, Watson & Viney Ltd, 1933).
p 122 Text B: from *Simply Spain*, 2000, Simply Travel Ltd.
p 122 Text C: from *The Hutchinson Dictionary of Science* edited by Peter Lafferty and Julian Rowe (Helicon, 1993).
p 122 Text A (lower): from *Dictionary of Twentieth Century World Biography* by Asa Briggs (OUP, 1992)
p 123 Text C: from 'Crunchy Bran' packaging, Weetabix Ltd.

Although we have tried to trace and contact all copyright holders, this has not always been possible. If notified, the publisher undertakes to rectify any errors or omissions at the earliest opportunity.

INTRODUCTION

Welcome to GCSE English/English Literature.

This book will help you to build the essential skills and knowledge to reach your potential in the GCSE English and English Literature exams. It gives you:

- an exact match to the requirements of the AQA/A examination papers
- short, confidence-building activities
- sample questions and answers
- comments from experienced Examiners
- a strong focus on language – this will help you to gain the highest marks
- guidelines on how to develop your writing skills – something that most books ignore
- hints and tips throughout
- a handy list of key words that you'll need throughout the course
- a strong model of learning throughout – building your confidence step-by-step, and placing you in control of your own progress.

It was an enjoyable book to write, and I'm grateful to my Year 10 and Year 11 students here in Suffolk who gave me feedback throughout the process.

Good luck with your GCSE English and English Literature exams. Using this book, I hope you even manage to enjoy preparing for them!

Geoff Barton

Key to icons

 spoken activity (pairs or small groups)

 spoken activity (full class)

 language activity

 reading activity

 writing activity

TO THE STUDENT

This book aims to help you achieve higher grades in English and
English Literature. It works like this:

- ●   Know what you need to learn and how you will be assessed

- ●   Check how good your skills already are

- ●   Develop your skills and practise them

- ●   Look at sample work and model answers from other students

- ●   Read the comments of the Examiner

- ●   Improve your skills. The book uses lots of short units to help
  you build your skills.

Getting started

Start by looking at the experiences and skills you'll need to do well at
GCSE English and English Literature . . .

MAPPING OUT YOUR ENGLISH COURSE

SPEAKING AND LISTENING (EN1)

Experiences	Skills you will develop and practise	How you will be assessed
explain, describe, narrate explore, analyse, imagine discuss, argue, persuade	communicate clearly and imaginatively, structuring and sustaining your talk and adapting it to different situations, using standard English appropriately; participate in discussion by both speaking and listening, judging the nature and purposes of contributions and the role of participants; adopt roles and communicate with audiences using a range of techniques	Spoken coursework which will include group interaction, a drama-focused activity and an extended individual contribution

READING (EN2)

Experiences	Skills you will develop and practise	How you will be assessed
a play by Shakespeare work from the English literary heritage by at least one major author texts from different cultures and traditions non-fiction texts (e.g. autobiographies, biographies, journals) media texts (e.g. magazines, newspapers, radio, television and film)	read, with insight and engagement, making appropriate references to texts and developing and sustaining interpretations of them; distinguish between fact and opinion and evaluate how information is presented; follow an argument, identifying implications and recognizing inconsistencies; select material appropriate to your purpose, collate material from different sources, and make cross references; understand and evaluate how writers use linguistic, structural, and presentational devices to achieve their effects, and comment on ways language varies and changes.	Shakespeare coursework Prose Study coursework Paper 1 Section A Non-fiction/media texts Paper 2 Section A Poetry from other cultures in the *Anthology*

WRITING (EN3)

Experiences	Skills you will develop and practise	How you will be assessed
Writing to: explore, imagine, entertain inform, explain, describe argue, persuade, advise analyse, review, comment	communicate clearly and imaginatively, using and adapting forms for different readers and purposes; organize ideas into sentences, paragraphs and whole texts using a variety of linguistic and structural features; use a range of sentence structures effectively with accurate punctuation and spelling	Media coursework Original Writing coursework Paper 1 Section B Argue, persuade, advise Paper 2 Section B Inform, explain, describe

GCSE ENGLISH SELF-EVALUATION PROFILE

How confident are you in this skill?
1 = not confident   2   3   4 = very confident

Come back to this document every half-term so that you can see at a glance how your skills and knowledge are developing.

SPEAKING & LISTENING	Half term 1	2	3	4	5	6
◆ communicate clearly and imaginatively, structuring and sustaining your talk and adapting it to different situations, using standard English appropriately ◆ participate in discussion by both speaking and listening, judging the nature and purposes of contributions and the role of participants ◆ adopt roles and communicate with audiences using a range of techniques						

READING	Half term 1	2	3	4	5	6
◆ read, with insight and engagement, making appropriate references to texts and developing and sustaining interpretations of them ◆ distinguish between fact and opinion and evaluate how information is presented ◆ follow an argument, identifying implications and recognizing inconsistencies ◆ select material appropriate to your purpose, collate material from different sources, and make cross references ◆ understand and evaluate how writers use linguistic, structural, and presentational devices to achieve their effects, and comment on ways language varies and changes.						

WRITING	Half term 1	2	3	4	5	6
◆ communicate clearly and imaginatively, using and adapting forms for different readers and purposes ◆ organize ideas into sentences, paragraphs and whole texts using a variety of linguistic and structural features ◆ use a range of sentence structures effectively with accurate punctuation and spelling						

MAPPING OUT YOUR ENGLISH LITERATURE COURSE

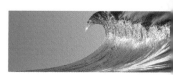

Skills you will develop and practise	How you will be assessed
Respond to texts critically, sensitively, and in detail, selecting appropriate ways to convey your response, using textual evidence as appropriate	Written paper Section A (prose) Written paper Section B (poetry) Pre-1914 Drama coursework Pre-1914 Prose coursework Post-1914 Drama coursework
Explore how language, structure, and forms contribute to the meanings of texts, considering different approaches to texts and alternative interpretations	Written paper Section A (prose) Written paper Section B (poetry) Pre-1914 Drama coursework Pre-1914 Prose coursework Post-1914 Drama coursework
Explore relationships and comparisons between texts, selecting and evaluating relevant material	Written paper Section B (poetry)
Relate texts to their social, cultural, and historical contexts and literary traditions	Pre-1914 Drama coursework Pre-1914 Prose coursework Post-1914 Drama coursework

1 NON-FICTION

How to study non-fiction texts

How to write autobiographical text

In this unit you will develop these skills:

SPEAKING AND LISTENING	READING	WRITING	LANGUAGE WORKSHOP
Extended individual piece	Reading non-fiction texts (journals, diaries, autobiographies)	Writing to inform, explain, describe	Comparing writers' styles
For coursework assessment of your spoken English	For English paper 1, section A	For English paper 2, section B	For English paper 1, section A

INTRODUCTION

Non-fiction texts are texts which are NOT fiction. In other words, they do not tell made-up stories (so they are not like novels, plays, and short stories).

Throughout your English GCSE course you need to be confident in reading all types of non-fiction texts, including

◆ non-fiction (e.g. journals, diaries, autobiographies) and
◆ media texts (e.g. newspapers, magazines, websites).

This unit explores non-fiction texts. Media texts are covered in Unit 2. To help you see the way the texts are written, the unit uses lots of short spoken and written activities. Then it gives you practice for the kinds of activities you will face in the final examination.

Activity 1 Looking at blogging

Human beings have used writing for thousands of years to express their thoughts and feelings. In the past we used diaries and journals. Now there is a new form. Read this article from BBC WebWise and use it to explore 'blogging':

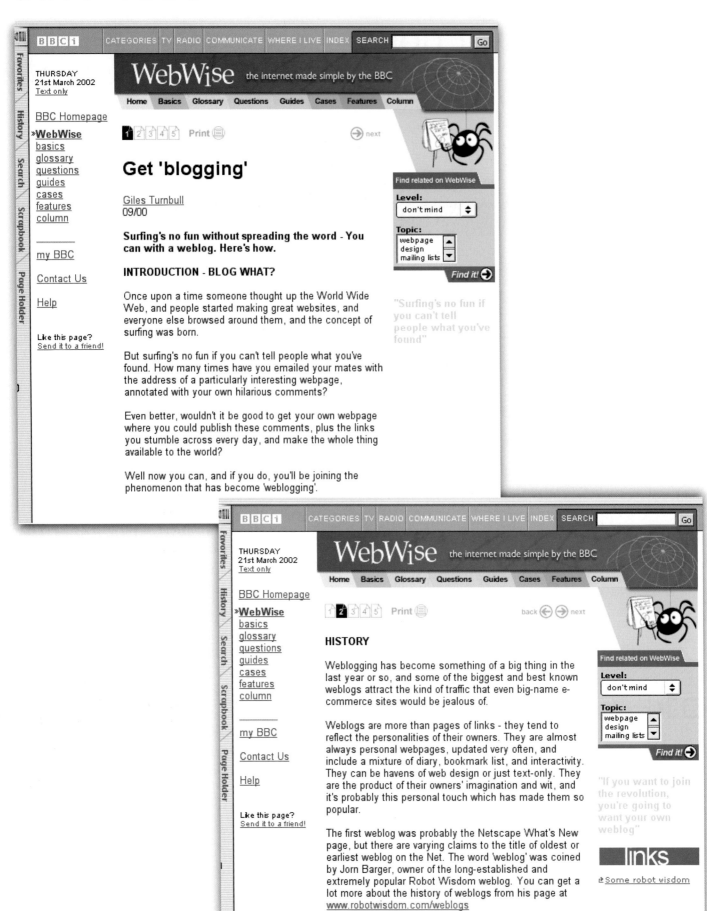

Get 'blogging'

Giles Turnbull
09/00

Surfing's no fun without spreading the word - You can with a weblog. Here's how.

INTRODUCTION - BLOG WHAT?

Once upon a time someone thought up the World Wide Web, and people started making great websites, and everyone else browsed around them, and the concept of surfing was born.

But surfing's no fun if you can't tell people what you've found. How many times have you emailed your mates with the address of a particularly interesting webpage, annotated with your own hilarious comments?

Even better, wouldn't it be good to get your own webpage where you could publish these comments, plus the links you stumble across every day, and make the whole thing available to the world?

Well now you can, and if you do, you'll be joining the phenomenon that has become 'weblogging'.

"Surfing's no fun if you can't tell people what you've found"

HISTORY

Weblogging has become something of a big thing in the last year or so, and some of the biggest and best known weblogs attract the kind of traffic that even big-name e-commerce sites would be jealous of.

Weblogs are more than pages of links - they tend to reflect the personalities of their owners. They are almost always personal webpages, updated very often, and include a mixture of diary, bookmark list, and interactivity. They can be havens of web design or just text-only. They are the product of their owners' imagination and wit, and it's probably this personal touch which has made them so popular.

The first weblog was probably the Netscape What's New page, but there are varying claims to the title of oldest or earliest weblog on the Net. The word 'weblog' was coined by Jorn Barger, owner of the long-established and extremely popular Robot Wisdom weblog. You can get a lot more about the history of weblogs from his page at www.robotwisdom.com/weblogs

"If you want to join the revolution, you're going to want your own weblog"

links

⇗ Some robot wisdom

Talking points

1   Think about what kind of text a weblog is. Use the text-type scale below to try to categorize it by comparing it to other types of non-fiction text. Try to place each text type on all of the scales:

Text type A: a leaflet about healthy eating
Text type B: a biography of Henry VIII published in a book
Text type C: a letter from a child thanking a grandparent for a
            birthday present
Text type D: a diary written during the London plague (1665)
Text type E: a weblog

private	1	2	3	public
personal style	1	2	3	impersonal style
fact	1	2	3	opinion
formal style	1	2	3	informal style
informative	1	2	3	entertaining

2   Which older texts types are weblogs most similar to? Which are they most different from? Explain why.

3   An adult says: 'I can't see the point of weblogs'. How would you explain their purpose? Write a paragraph giving your response.

Activity 2   Writing about ourselves

Apart from weblogs, people use notebooks to record their thoughts and feelings. Sometimes these are in diaries (an entry written to record events each day). Sometimes they are called journals. 'Journal' means 'every day' (from the French word *jour*), but journals are often longer texts in which people reflect more on how they are feeling.

Many diaries and journals are written in secret. Explore more about the way they work.

Talking points

- Do you agree with this statement?
- Is it possible for writing to be truly private?

Discuss a time when you have used writing to help you think about things that have happened to you, to try to sort out worries, or to put your thoughts in order before attempting a task.

'If someone writes a diary or journal they can't be writing it only for themselves. They must know that someone might read it one day. Otherwise they wouldn't write it down – they'd just think it!'

Dan, Year 10

When you write privately, how does your style change? Do you:

- write in sentences
- write in poetry
- scribble

- ◆ doodle
- ◆ use abbreviations or codes
- ◆ use bullet points
- ◆ list words and ideas at random
- ◆ consider how you should express your ideas
- ◆ consider whether someone might see what you have written?

Talk in a small group about your attitude to private writing.

LANGUAGE WORKSHOP

The text below is a tangle of three different types of writing, all written in wartime:

Text 1: A diary written by Kitty Kenyon, a nurse in France during WW1 (written 9 August 1918)

Text 2: A letter written by G. Crompton, a Lieutenant in the Napoleonic Wars (1811)

Text 3: An autobiography written by William Gibney, a British Army surgeon at the Battle of Waterloo (1815)

Sentences from the different texts have been mixed together. Each sentence is labelled to help you re-organize it. Try to work out which sentence belongs to which text.

Then think about how you were able to tell which sentence belonged to which text.

Clues to look for:
- ◆ Does the language seem to be addressed to a separate reader, or is it being written for the writer him- or herself?
- ◆ Does the writer use stock phrases used in letters (e.g. Dear . . .)?
- ◆ Are there any clues that one text may have been written longer ago?
- ◆ Does the text feel more like a story than a reflection?
- ◆ How far can you work out which text is which by looking at the content (what the text is about) rather than from language clues?

A On the night of 10th there was a raid and through it the theatre was working and patients being brought back to the wards by steel-hatted stretcher bearers.

B A few lines my dearest mother, I, in haste, sit down and write, to say, that under the protection of Almighty God, I have escaped unhurt in one of the severest actions that ever was contested between France and England; to describe the Horrors that were witnessed on the ever memorable 16th of May would be impossible.

C I had not been ten minutes in the village, indeed had hardly commenced giving my assistance, when the Colonel of my regiment was brought in desperately wounded.

D We had convoy after convoy, mostly Australians . . . But there's no anxiety these days – how different from last year!

E Give my most affectionate and kindest love to my Father, Annie, William, and all at home, and believe me to be your most affectionate son.

Use a grid like this to write down which sentence belongs to which text and how you can tell. Write the sentence label (A to E) here.
Write down some reasons for your decisions here – what were the main clues as to which sentence belonged where?

Text 1 – a diary (1918)	Text 2 – a letter (1811)	Text 3 – an autobiography (1815)

Activity 3 Texts in time

Autobiographies are texts in which people write about their own lives. Usually people write them when they are older and are looking back on their achievements. Recently, however, some media celebrities have written autobiographies before they have reached a third of the way through their lives.

This activity explores autobiographical writing.

Talking point

1 Why do you think people write autobiographies?
2 Why do you think people read autobiographies?
3 Why do you think people might read the autobiography of a music or sports star who is not yet aged 25?

Here are two extracts from autobiographies.
1 For each text, see what you can tell about:

◆ who is writing
◆ what they are writing about

Text A *It was on a bright day of midwinter, in New York. The little girl who eventually became me, but as yet was neither me nor anybody else in particular, but merely a soft anonymous morsel of humanity — this little girl, who bore my name, was going for a walk with her father. The episode is literally the first thing I can remember about her, and therefore I date the birth of her humanity from that day.*

Text B *I remember being taken, when I was about four years old, with two cousins of my age, up the hill, past the semi-detached houses, past the larger and older ones with carriage gates and gate-stop latches that clicked, over the railway bridge, up again past the last houses of all, and I remember being lifted over a fence between oak trees into a field of buttercups. At first we just stood. For a few moments the world stood still with us.*

2   How much do the paragraphs make you want to keep reading on? Try to explain why.

3   The two texts show how literary non-fiction texts are different from purely informative texts. If writer A had simply wanted to inform, she might have written:

   At the age of 6, I remember going for a walk in New York with my father. This is my first memory.

   Take text B. Rewrite it as a purely informative text. What is missing from the new version?

4   Literary non-fiction often uses language that interests or surprises us. For example, writers might:

   ◆ use unusual vocabulary
   ◆ refer to the senses (sound, touch, etc.) to help bring a memory to life
   ◆ use very short or very long sentences for effect
   ◆ use an unexpected pronoun (e.g. *she/her* instead of *I/me*)

The result can be writing which is more interesting but also more complex.

Look at these examples of language use from both texts. Using the checklist of style features above and a grid like the one below, think about how both writers make their language interesting.

Then, for the third column, think of how the writer could have expressed the same idea in a different way (e.g. making the language simpler). Decide whether you prefer your rewritten version or the original.

Example of interesting language	What makes the language interesting?	Which version do you prefer – the original, or your rewritten version? Try to say why
'The little girl who eventually became me, but as yet was neither me nor anybody else in particular'		
'soft anonymous morsel of humanity'		
'I date the birth of her humanity from that day.'		
'gate-stop latches that clicked'		
'For a few moments the world stood still with us.'		

Activity 4 Building your writing skills

This activity gets you exploring autobiographical writing actively. It uses a spoken task and then a writing task to help you explore the way people present autobiographical information.

The Radio 4 programme 'Desert Island Discs' asks guests to decide which songs, book, and personal item they would take with them to a desert island. Think about:

- a book that has influenced you
- a song that reminds you of a time in your past
- an object which is important to you

⊣ H I N T S ⊢

Book

Choose a book that you have read and re-read, one that made an impact on you when you first read it. It might be a book you read when you were learning to read. Talk about the memories of reading it with someone else or hearing it read aloud. It may be a book you read on your own when older. It may be an old-fashioned book now, but it will have caught your imagination when young.

Song

Choose a song from your past, one that reminds you of a particular time or place – e.g. a holiday or school trip. This song may not have been a favourite song – in fact, you may find it embarrassing and silly – but it conjures up strong memories which are either happy or sad.

Object

This might be something from your childhood – an old teddy-bear – or something you have acquired since. It might be something given to you by a relative, or a special present.

Talking point

Start by discussing your items in a small group, or use them as the basis of a class talk. You could use this to be assessed on an 'extended individual contribution' for your English spoken coursework.

If you choose the class talk, aim to speak for three to five minutes about yourself – who you are now, and how you have developed from the person you were in the past.

Use the three items to help you express your thoughts. Don't bring anything valuable into school. You could simply talk about it instead.

Whether you have chosen group interaction or the formal talk, use the advice panel below to help you organize your ideas. Look at the examples to help get the right tone (not too formal, not too informal).

Advice	Example
Introduction Tell your listeners what you will be talking about. This will help to provide a clear structure.	My talk covers three different parts of my life. I'm going to show you a book from when I was around five. It's one of my earliest memories. Then I'll play you part of a really embarrassing song that I used to listen to when I was in the car with my parents. I was probably about eight or nine. Then . . .
Book Hold up the book. Say what it is about. Describe the characters. Read out a sample paragraph. Say what you remember best about it. Talk about the look and feel of the book.	This is my book. It's an Enid Blyton story that I read several times. It looks a bit battered these days. That's because my sister read it before I did. It's part of our family's collection of paperbacks. It's all about a group of children called . . .

Song Introduce the song. Say specifically what memories it conjures up. Say what you like / dislike about it. Try to say something about the lyrics and the musical production (i.e. how it sounds). Play an extract. Read out some of the words. Help us to imagine what you were like when you used to listen to it.	My song is a really embarrassing one. It's not really a song I ever liked, but it's one of those songs that gets inside your mind and haunts you. I first heard it with my family when we went on holiday to Tenerife. It was our first holiday there and I was really disappointed when we first arrived because it was cloudy. We decided to head down to the hotel bar, and this song was playing . . .
Object This might be from your past, or you might use it to talk about the person you are today. It might be a serious present from a friend, or something silly that you keep on display at home. Say something about the object, what you like about its looks and texture. Comment on the memories it conjures up. Talk about the person / people it reminds you of.	Finally, my object is a small diary given to me by my grandmother some years ago. It contains memories she wrote down when she was growing up. For example, here she says . . .
Conclusion Round your talk off by saying something about your life so far: best moments and worst moments; times that have changed you; what kind of person you are now and how you expect to be in the next few years.	So that's my talk. As you can see my life so far has been pretty unexciting and fairly happy. Many of the best points seem to have been before I was ten. The worst time was definitely . . . Thanks for listening. Are there any questions?

Hints on delivery

1 You will not be allowed to script and read out your talk. Use cue-cards if you wish, but once you have organized the structure of the talk, you shouldn't need too many notes. It needs to sound personal and friendly, so a few hesitations will be fine.

2 Look at the audience as you speak. Try to stand still and hold each item as you talk. Don't hide behind notes.

3 Use connectives to help your listener follow the structure:

In my talk I will . . .
First . . .
Next . . .
Now . . .
Finally . . .

Now use the same approach to structure an autobiographical essay. Think about:

◆ an opening sentence that introduces the topic – for example, 'If I suddenly found myself on a desert island . . .'
◆ using a general opening paragraph followed by three paragraphs which focus on the book, song, and object
◆ how you will link the different sections of the personal writing together – for example: 'For my special object I would choose . . .'

Activity 5 Building your reading skills

The basics

Paper 1 assesses your response to non-fiction and media texts. You will need to be able to show your reading skills.

In section A you will be asked to look in detail at two or more texts. One of these is a media text (see Unit 2). The other is a non-fiction text.

To respond successfully to the non-fiction text, you will need to be able to:

◆ understand what is being said
◆ comment on the content and style
◆ compare the text with the media text, looking at content, language, and use of layout

Practise reading and responding to non-fiction using this extract.

Fergal Keane writes each week for the *Independent* newspaper. He is also a special correspondent with the BBC. In this edited extract, he reflects on how to celebrate Christmas, following the Twin Towers tragedy of September 11, 2001.

Glossary

Commercialism and materialism – celebrating spending money and getting possessions
Intrinsic – in-built
Pandemonium – chaos
Urbi et Orbi – (Latin): to the city and the world
Riposte – answer

Talking point

Before you read Fergal Keane's article, discuss this viewpoint:

'The attack on the New York Twin Towers was one of the most terrible events in recent years. Therefore it would have been wrong for people to treat Christmas 2001 as just another Christmas. Instead people should have made it a much quieter occasion, without all the usual glitz.'

- What do you think?
- Should people have changed the way they celebrated Christmas 2001?

Now read Fergal Keane's article.

01 December 2001

Fergal Keane: 'Tis the season to be as merry as possible

'Have fun, and to hell with the glums. The ability to have fun without cruelty is a benchmark of civilisation.'

. . . If ever there was a time when we needed to enjoy the good things in life, it is this Christmas of 2001. And please let it be a season in which we do not have to endure the great annual whinge about commercialism and materialism . . .

There is nothing wrong in spending money you haven't stolen. (Though I am assured by those who know that there is a great pleasure in spending money you have stolen). I adore the sound of the Christmas streets, glutted with shoppers and awash with money. This is not because I have any intrinsic love of money. I don't. But I love the sense of bonds being broken, the saved money of a year escaping across the counter, the budgetary restraint of 12 prior months exploding in one great spree. My friends, go out and have fun, and to hell with the glums. It doesn't mean you are careless or callous, rather the opposite. The ability to have fun without cruelty to others is a benchmark of civilisation.

As a child in an alcoholic home I sat through some grim Christmases and I know that for many the season is one of fear and desolation. But I always loved the strange magic of the season; it was something no amount of drunken rages could destroy. Our Christmases were divided between the city and the country. At the risk of lapsing into 'McCourtese' (the most lucrative and lachrymose of all Irish literary traditions), let me offer you

some images of those days: the lanes off Henry Street in Dublin bustling like a fabulous bazaar, crowded with old women who hawked gaudy decorations and cheap toys to the city's poor; a John Field nocturne trembling from our first rickety record player as my mother wrapped presents on Christmas Eve; a roasted goose sitting on my grandmother's kitchen table in County Kerry, steam rising from a pile of potatoes the height of Mount Brandon; the St Stephens Day Wren Boys wreathed in straw, their faces blacked, singing and dancing on the street outside her door; a night going back to Kerry in Christmas week when we got lost in fog and slept in the car, a world I recognised from the writing of Patrick Kavanagh:

A water-hen screeched in the bog,
mass-going feet crunched the wafer
ice on the pot-holes,
somebody wistfully twisted the
bellows wheel.
My child poet picked out the letters
on the grey stone,
In silver the wonder of Christmas
townland,
the winking glitter of a frosty dawn.

Now that I must shepherd a five-year-old boy through Christmas I am caught up again in the whirling energy of downtown streets, overseeing the writing of a letter to the North Pole and counting the days to a morning of gifts and bacon sandwiches. These last have been a family ritual since time began. As a child I used to wake around four o'clock on Christmas morning. My own son has inherited the habit. This Christmas I will sit down to lunch with 17 people in a house in County Clare. I have no doubt it will be chaotic. Red-faced and overtired children will first play and then do battle. When I say that they range in age from six months to 14 years you may be tempted to sympathise, or at least murmur: 'Thank God it's not me.'

Too many people will crowd the kitchen offering unwanted advice. Some vital ingredient will be discovered missing and the only shop in town will be closing in five minutes. The men will congregate in the hall, blocking the way, and talk hurling and football. My father-in-law will sit serenely at the head of the table, nursing a glass of Jamesons, blissfully untroubled by the pandemonium.

I won't even attempt to get a word in at the table. It would be foolish to compete with my voluble and beloved in-laws. It will be a brilliant day. In all of this how much time will be devoted to the spiritual aspect of Christmas? There will be a convoy to Mass and the children will put on a nativity play. The Irish television news will broadcast Pope John Paul's Christmas message. Urbi et Orbi. More of our customary rhythms. On the surface it may not look like a great spiritual commitment. But the surface is a place for lazy minds. If you are among those you love and can laugh with them that is spirit enough, a fit riposte to hatred and war.

Exploring the text

FOUNDATION

1 What do we learn about the writer from this extract?
2 What picture does he create of a traditional Christmas?
3 What arguments does he give for celebrating Christmas in the way he is accustomed to?

HIGHER

1 What do we learn about the writer from this extract?
2 How does the writer use language to make the Christmas scenes vivid?
3 What arguments does he give for celebrating Christmas in the way he is accustomed to?

Advice:

◆ Answer in short paragraphs.
◆ Leave a space between each answer to help the examiner read them all clearly.
◆ Avoid being too personal. Don't write 'I think that . . .'. Instead put 'The writer says . . .', 'Fergal Keane shows . . .'
◆ Support your points with examples.

For top marks . . .

Structure your answers so they include a point (from you), some evidence (a quotation or specific reference to something in the text), and then a comment by you on the quotation. Try to say something about the writer's use of language in every answer.

Activity 6 Getting the style of your answers right

The ways you express your thoughts and ideas in an examination are vital. However good your reading skills, you need to get your ideas down on paper clearly and accurately.

This activity helps you to improve your writing skills in exam conditions.

Compare a skilful answer with a less successful one. These answers are in response to Question 1:

1 What do we learn about the writer from this extract?

Answer 1	Answer 2
The writer likes Christmas and he thinks we should keep celebrating it because people need to be happy even though it's a miserable time.	The writer was brought up in Ireland where he had some 'grim' Christmases. Nevertheless he recalls the 'strange magic of the season' which, as an adult, he hopes to pass on to his child. We learn quite a lot about his background – the people and places of his memory. We also learn that he is someone of strong opinions who is not afraid to say what he thinks. Also, despite the 'grimness' of some of his memories, the writer is an optimist. He says 'it will be a brilliant day'. He evidently enjoys the chaos of family Christmases.

1 What is wrong with this answer? Think about:
  ♦ the content
  ♦ the use of sentences
  ♦ the use of vocabulary
	2 What is good about this answer?
	3 Could it be improved?

Once you have looked at the two answers, read the Examiner's comments upon them:

Answer 1	Answer 2
This is: ♦ Too brief. ♦ It doesn't really answer the question. It tells us about the writer's opinions, but not about the writer. ♦ The single long sentence feels a bit rambling. It would be better as two shorter sentences. ♦ The vocabulary could be more ambitious – for example, a different word instead of *miserable*.	This is: ♦ Very impressive. ♦ Well structured (early points about the writer's past; later points about the writer now). ♦ Organized clearly using connectives (e.g. *nevertheless, also, despite*). ♦ Good vocabulary (e.g. *despite*). ♦ Impressive use of embedded quotations (i.e. built in to the student's answers rather than tagged on separately).

Work likely to produce an E grade candidate

Work likely to produce an A grade candidate

Use this feedback to write answers to the other two questions on page 12.

2 MEDIA TEXTS

In this unit you will develop these skills:

SPEAKING AND LISTENING	READING	WRITING	LANGUAGE WORKSHOP
Discussing fact v. opinion	Reading a range of media texts – in particular newspapers	Writing to inform, explain, describe (the text type of newspaper reporting)	Using features of newspapers: ◆ headlines ◆ topic sentences ◆ paragraphing ◆ connectives
For coursework assessment of your contribution to a group discussion	For English paper 1, section A	For English paper 2, section B	For English paper 1 and paper 2

INTRODUCTION

Media texts include:

- ◆ newspaper articles
- ◆ magazine articles
- ◆ leaflets
- ◆ websites

Start by thinking about what media texts are.

Activity 1   Exploring media texts

1   This collection of mystery texts has been printed as plain text only. See if you can work out which is:

- ◆ a newspaper article
- ◆ a magazine article
- ◆ a leaflet

A Pop star George Michael is back on the music scene in a big way, starring in one of the most expensive music videos ever made. The £1 million clip for Freeek, which marks his return to the medium after a three-year absence, sees the Outside singer don £80,000 worth of costumes . . .

B Bullfighting:
Ban the business
Every year more than 30,000 bulls die a cruel and painful death in Spanish bullrings.

C SCIENTISTS have extracted DNA from a dodo to find its closest relative.

The life 'blueprint' was taken from one of the flightless birds donated to Oxford University in 1683, two years after it was last sighted.

2 Media texts like these use **layout** features to communicate. Draw **three** quick sketches, using no words, to show what the format of the text type would look like.

The format of a newspaper page looks like this . . .	The format of a magazine page looks like this . . .	The format of a leaflet looks like this . . .

3 Based on your three sketches, write down what you think are the essential ingredients that make the layout of the three text types different:

a) The essential layout ingredients of a newspaper page are . . .
b) The essential layout ingredients of a magazine page are . . .
c) The essential layout ingredients of a leaflet are . . .

Activity 2 Looking at audience

1 Imagine someone asks you 'how is a newspaper different from a magazine?' What do you say?

2 How much of your answer was about layout or format? Without mentioning these, how is a newspaper different from a magazine? Use these prompts to structure your thinking:

◆ the purpose of a magazine might be different from the purpose of a newspaper because . . .
◆ the audience of a magazine might be different from the audience of a newspaper because . . .
◆ the language of a magazine might be different from the language of a newspaper because . . .

The audience of a magazine might have a special interest in a topic or want to find out more about the topic.

How can you tell by looking at the language of a text whether the audience is general or specialist?

A general audience may have some interest in the topic but is not an expert.
A specialist audience already knows a lot about the topic and may be an expert.

Here are three examples of text taken from three sources:

- one is from *Practical Fishkeeping* magazine
- one is from a website designed to teach children about fish
- one is from a research report by a university expert on fish

- Which do you expect to be more straightforward to follow?
- Which do you think will use the most technical language?

See whether you can work out which text is which.

A
If you've ever tried to grow aquatic plants and failed then Julian Whinyates' set-up will make you very envious … When he decided to go for the larger set-up, using a 4' Juwel Rio 240, Julian had the tank hood and stand built to match the furniture he'd already got, in real mahogany.

Julian uses Aquaponics substor on the tank base with a layer of quartz gravel on top. It's a good thick substrate – around 4–5' in depth.

He is also a great believer in the benefits of using CO_2 in a planted aquarium.

B
Speciation is the process by which a single evolutionary lineage becomes more than one lineage. Speciation is one of the main mechanisms generating biodiversity. Like many fish groups, gymnotiform species diversity is not distributed uniformly throughout the Amazon basin. Upland forest streams and tributary headwaters exhibit a low alpha yet high beta diversity profile. This means relatively few species inhabit each particular locality, but there is a large amount of turnover in species composition between localities. The opposite pattern is observed on the floodplains, where many species co-exist and each species has a more extensive range.

C How old are salmon when they migrate from freshwater to the ocean?

That depends on the species:

Chinook: fall chinook, 3–4 months after hatch; spring chinook, 12–16 months

Coho – 12–24 months

Chum – 1 week to a month

Sockeye – 12 months to 36 months

Pink – 1 week to a month

How do salmon find their way back home to spawn after being out at sea?

They follow their noses. Salmon are able to detect the scent of their home stream and follow it upriver.

1   What helped you work out the differences between the different text types?

2   Which words helped you to work out what each text was?

3   What clues were there in the types or lengths of sentences?

Activity 3   Getting the audience level right

- Look at this longer extract from the information, which is aimed at children. Do you think it is easy enough for most children to understand?
- Look at the level of vocabulary. Is it too difficult?
- How might you change some of the language to make the text easier for children aged 8–12 to understand?

Have a go at bringing the language level of this paragraph down:

Is it true that salmon return to spawn in freshwater areas where they were born?

Almost always. Some straying has been documented, but it is minor. Most spawning salmon return to the precise stream of their birth, sometimes overcoming great distances and hazardous river conditions to reach home.

What is a kokanee, or silver trout?

It is the landlocked subspecies of a sockeye salmon. The kokanee spends its entire life in fresh water and usually does not attain the size of its sea-migrating cousin.

Designing layouts

These tasks are designed to prepare you for looking at layouts in your Reading work. Imagine you have been asked to present information about salmon for a young audience. Your job is as the designer, not the writer. You are presented with the text and it is your job to make it look visually interesting so that the audience finds it clear and enjoyable to read.

How would you approach the task if you were . . .

a) designing the text for a magazine page?
b) designing the text for a website page?

Look at the designer's briefing memo and then draw up two quick designs to show what the texts would look like.

Memo

Re: magazine

This is a general interest magazine for 8–12 year olds. It contains features on films, books, music, and hobbies. The idea here is to get the audience interested in where fish live, how they are caught, and how we need to take care to preserve fishing stocks. The style needs to be lively but informative.

Memo

Re: website

This will be a page of a website aimed at young people. It aims to make them more environmentally aware. Fish are currently being hunted to extinction and we want this page to tell them more of the facts about the fishing industry. It needs to be a dramatic page which is also interactive and allows readers easily to follow their interests to other pages and sites.

─┤ H I N T S ├─

- Think of headings and headlines. You don't need to write in any other text. The idea is to show the layout.
- Draw a quick sketch to show where you want images to go. Label these to say 'photo of salmon' or 'cartoon of smiling fish' but don't worry about drawing anything carefully.
- Use horizontal lines to show where the main text would go.

For the magazine, remember you could use:

- short paragraphs
- sub-headings
- captions (labels beneath photos)
- bullet points
- diagrams and images

For the website, remember you could use:

◆ short paragraphs
◆ sub-headings
◆ captions (labels beneath photos)
◆ bullet points
◆ diagrams and images
◆ hypertext (underlined words which link to other pages/sites)
◆ animations
◆ interactive games

Underneath each of your designs, write a brief paragraph explaining your approach and the design decisions you have made. You might start like this:

My magazine page aims to catch the reader's interest by . . .

EXPLORING NEWSPAPERS

Introduction

Newspapers are designed to inform and entertain us. They usually contain a mixture of:

◆ news ◆ gossip ◆ advertising
◆ information ◆ opinion

Activity 4 How NOT to write a newspaper story

Look at the panel below. It tells the story of two men who almost died in an avalanche. It is also VERY BORING.

Working in pairs or small groups, read the story and think about what is wrong with it.

Big avalanche nearly killed two people

Yesterday a big avalanche nearly killed two people who were out enjoying a walk on a mountainside in Scotland, but they were lucky that although they did get hurt quite a lot at least they survived.

The two men were called Peter Clarke and Peter Clarke. Peter Clarke is Peter Clarke's father. He is 46 and his son is 28.

They were very lucky not to get badly injured or even killed . . .

Tasks

1 Why is the text so boring . . . ? Brainstorm five features
   that make the newspaper story so dull to read.
2 Working quickly, decide what you would do to . . .
a) improve the layout
b) improve the headline
c) improve the first sentence

Activity 5 Advice on how to write newspaper articles

Read this advice from journalist James Radcliff.

James Radcliff's five top hints for journalists:

1 Think of your audience. They don't have much time. They
want their news to be easy-to-read and dramatic. So think
of a good headline, with short punchy words (not too many
syllables), plenty of drama (words like *crash, horror, shock*),
and always in the present tense (*kills* not *killed*).

2 Your first sentence should tell the whole story. It's known as
the topic sentence. It will usually answer the questions
Who? Where? What? When? Why? Put the important bits
of information (who . . .) at the start of the sentence. Put
the least important bits (when . . .) at the end.

3 Keep your paragraphs short – usually just one or two
sentences long. Use labels to squeeze in as much
information as possible (Scottish mountainside, rather
than a mountainside in Scotland – it uses fewer words).

4 Remember that your readers want to know about people's
feelings. Give them comments and quotations from
eyewitnesses. Help them to see what it was like to be there.

5 Don't waste words. If you don't need a word, cut it out.

Good luck!

James Radcliff

Use James Radcliff's advice to write . . .

a) a better headline for the avalanche story
b) a better first sentence

Activity 6 Exploring a real newspaper story

The avalanche story was reported in *Metro*, a free newspaper published each weekday in London and other big UK cities.

Read the story, looking at the way the writer makes it dramatic and interesting. Then use the prompts which follow to discuss fact v. opinion and the way the story is put together.

Inches from tragedy

BY DAVID FICKLING

WHERE THE AVALANCHE HIT

1. Avalanche triggered by Andrew Clark who was leading his brother and nephew. His feet dislodged a snow overhang.

902ft

2. Peter Clark and his son hit by the 20ft wide slab of snow and fell almost 500ft. They stopped only 12ft from the edge of boulder-studded slope.

Glencoe

A82

Glasgow

Avalanche occurred on Stob Dearg. Temp was −4°C but with winds of 25mph in some areas, it felt as low as −10°C.

Andrew Clark   Peter Clark

A FATHER and son who were swept 500ft down a mountainside by an avalanche told yesterday how they escaped death by inches.

Peter Clark, 46, and his 28-year-old son, also called Peter, were hit by a wall of snow and ice and slithered to a halt feet from the edge of a steep, boulder-studded slope.

The pair were walking with Mr Clark Snr's brother, Andrew, 35, on Sunday when when he accidentally triggered the snow slide.

As he reached the highest point of the Buachaille Etive Mor in the Scottish Highlands, a 20ft wide section of snow broke away and crashed into his relatives below, sweeping them off their feet.

'I watched them tumble down the hill but then the momentum of the snow slowed and they stopped only a few feet from going further down the corrie,' he said.

His nephew, a finance company underwriter from Radcliffe-on-Trent, Nottinghamshire, said: 'It is hard to believe it was only 500ft we fell because it seemed an eternity until I stopped.

'There was no warning and me and dad had no chance to jump clear before we were off down the hill being battered by lumps of ice.

'I was told by the rescuers that we were lucky because as avalanches go it was quite a small one and we were not buried.

'I remember my arms and legs being all over the place and I think that is how I suffered a puncture wound to one of my knees from my crampons.'

His father, a BT manager from Wilford, Nottinghamshire, broke his ankle.

Their fall was seen by a climbing instructor and member of Glencoe's Mountain Rescue Team, Mark Tenant, who called for help.

The injured pair were stretchered down the mountain and then airlifted to hospital.

Mr Tenant said: 'When I saw them tumble down the mountainside I was concerned for their lives.

'But luckily they both ended up on the surface of the snow. They were both pretty cheerful considering what they had been through and very relieved to be alive.'

Article from the Metro, Tuesday, 23 January, 2001

Look at the way the writer uses fact and opinion in this newspaper story.

E X A M   H I N T

You will need to become confident in telling facts from opinions. Paper 1 of the English exam tests this skill.

- Facts are statements that can be proved to be true (e.g. penguins have two legs).
- Opinions are statements made by someone that cannot so easily be proved (e.g. cooked penguins are delicious). Watch out for opinions disguised as facts!

1 Quickly re-read the text and make a list of:

Facts	Opinions

2   Discuss:

Are there more facts or opinions in the article?
Why do you think this is?

LANGUAGE WORKSHOP

Exploring newspaper style

E X A M   H I N T

You will need to become familiar with the style and layout of
newspapers and other non-fiction text-types. Paper 1 tests this in the
reading section. You will also need to be able to write in different
non-fiction styles (e.g. journalism, letter, persuasive leaflet and so
on). Paper 1 will test this in the writing section.

1   Think back to James Radcliff's advice on journalism. He says:

'the topic sentence . . . will usually answer the questions *Who? Where?
What? When?* and *Why?*'

Look at the topic sentence in this story. Use a chart like the one below
to write down which of the *wh-* questions it answers:

Who?	Where?	When?	What?	Why?

2   James Radcliff advises journalists: 'Remember that your readers
   want to know about people's feelings. Give them comments and
   quotations from eyewitnesses.'
a)   Which different people in the avalanche article are quoted?
b)   Is there anyone else whose comment might have been included?
   Explain why or why not.
3   The writer uses connectives to link ideas together. Here are some
   of the connectives he uses:

   also   and   when   as   but

Take paragraph three:

'The pair were walking with Mr Clark Snr's brother, Andrew, 35, on
Sunday when he accidentally triggered the snow slide.'

a)   Write this sentence as two shorter sentences which do NOT use
   the connective *when*.

How does this change the effect of the text?

b)   Write the sentence using a co-ordinating connective (*and, but* or
   or) instead of the subordinating connective *when*.

How does this change the effect of the text?

Activity 7 Building your reading skills

Read the article below from the *Bury St Edmunds Citizen*, a weekly free newspaper given out in parts of Suffolk.

Then use the questions which follow to see how well you have built your understanding of newspaper writing.

FIREMEN FREE BATHROOM TOT

By Joanne Green

A 15-month-old boy had to be rescued by fire officers after he accidentally locked himself in a bathroom.

Travis Tyler, of Kirkstead Road, Bury St Edmunds, was playing a game with his mother Tracey at just after 9.30am on Saturday when he ran into the bathroom and closed the door.

When Tracey tried to open the door minutes later she discovered that Travis has slipped the bolt, making it impossible for him to get out.

After she failed to open the door herself, Tracey called the fire brigade and Bury's Red Watch were on the scene within minutes.

Fire officers then set about getting the bathroom door open to free the mischievous youngster as quickly as possible.

"My dad had gone out so I couldn't ask him to try and open the door and my mum and I decided the only thing to do was to call the fire brigade for help," explained Tracey. "They were here very quickly and were wonderful," she added.

After levering the door frame away, fire officers used a hacksaw to cut through the door bolt. Their work was occasionally hampered by an inquisitive Travis, who was very interested in the hacksaw and had to be warned not to play with it.

Just before 10am the door lock was finally opened, revealing a bemused Travis, who had no idea what all the fuss was about.

Leading firefighter Peter Chaplain said: "The little boy had locked the latch which was just below the door handle so we took off the trim around the side of the door and then used a hacksaw to cut off the lock.

"It was good to get him out but I think he was a bit scared to see us in the end," he laughed.

Tracey added, "The firemen gave him a helmet and he had a good look at the fire engine."

E X A M   H I N T

Remember that you and your teacher will need to decide whether you will sit the foundation or higher tier exam paper.

Foundation tier lets you achieve grades G to C
Higher tier lets you achieve grades D to A*

FOUNDATION

1 Write down **three** facts we learn from the newspaper story
2 What are the **three** main points of this story?
3 Read the whole story. How does the writer make the story interesting by the use of:

 ◆ headlines
 ◆ dramatic and exciting language
 ◆ other presentational devices including pictures?

HIGHER

1   How does the writer make the story slightly comical? Choose **three** examples and comment on them.

2   How effectively does the writer of this article hold the reader's interest? Choose and write down **three** details and explain why they are effective.

3   Read the whole story. How does the writer make the story interesting by the use of:

  ◆   headlines
  ◆   dramatic and exciting language
  ◆   other presentational devices including pictures?

Activity 8   Building your writing skills

Imagine the following incident:

  ◆   A hot air balloon has to make an emergency landing on your school field, playground, or roof.
  ◆   There is a problem with the burners, but the pilot and six passengers manage to escape.
  ◆   Students are evacuated to another part of the school site and no one is hurt.
  ◆   The fire brigade and police are called.

Write a 200-word article for the local newspaper, **informing** your readers and **describing** what happens. Aim to:

  ◆   make your writing factual
  ◆   use an appropriate style for a local newspaper

─┤ H I N T S ├─

Spend time brainstorming your story. Think of:

  ◆   a good headline (short, punchy words; no more than seven words; cut any unnecessary words)
  ◆   names for: pilot, passengers, eyewitnesses.
  ◆   comments/statements from them that could be included

Start planning your story, starting with:

  ◆   a topic sentence that says *who, where, when, what* and *why*
  ◆   short paragraphs that add further detail
  ◆   connectives to join ideas, such as *when, as, then, later, earlier, although*
  ◆   comments from eyewitnesses to add opinion as well as fact

  ➡   To see a sample student answer, with examiner's comments and final grade, see page 25.
  ➡   To explore fact v. opinion, see page 21.
  ➡   To investigate other non-fiction styles, see page 1.

SAMPLE ANSWER

Writing a newspaper article

Read the answer on the left-hand side of the page, keeping the Examiner's comments covered. Decide what you think about the answer first.

Sample answer by Vicky, Year 10	Comments by Examiner
Balloon pitches on school roof By Vicky Oldknow A hot air balloon dropped onto the roof of a school yesterday and almost caused a great deal of damage. Pupils and staff at Stantonbury High School, Stanton, could not believe their eyes as they saw the balloon moving closer to the school. Headteacher Mike Foley said: 'It was like a slow-motion movie. The balloon just kept on coming. We thought it might be a joke but decided to evacuate the school building. I'm glad we did.' Year 8 pupil Sam Chapman-Allan said: 'It certainly made Maths more interesting'. The balloon was on a day's leisure tour and contained six fee-paying passengers who had wanted to see the Suffolk countryside from the air. When the pilot, Des Bowler, noticed a problem with the burners, he had no choice but to do an emergency landing. He said: 'It was embarrassing, but I couldn't see anywhere apart from the flat roof of the school. I was just very relieved that no one got hurt.' A spokesman for the local fire brigade said: 'We were impressed with how calm everyone was.'	This is a very good article. The headline is short, dramatic and to-the-point. It catches the reader's attention. The writer uses a topic sentence to introduce the whole story. It is good – except for the second part, 'a great deal of damage', which sounds a bit less dramatic. It sounds more like the writer's opinion than a fact. She might have said 'narrowly avoiding disaster' or something similarly dramatic. The writer uses facts and opinions well, though I think she goes into eyewitness statements a bit too early. She could have given more description of the event first. In places the tone is perhaps a bit jokey (for example, the comment about Maths). It could have had a comment from the passengers. Overall, it is a well-constructed piece of writing. The ideas are very effectively linked (notice the use of connective *when*). Work likely to be produced by a B grade candidate

3 POST-1914 PROSE

WILLIAM GOLDING, *Lord of the Flies*

In this unit you will develop these skills:

SPEAKING AND LISTENING	READING	WRITING	LANGUAGE WORKSHOP
Discussing different interpretations of the text	Reading *Lord of the Flies* to explore plot, character, themes, and language	Writing about *Lord of the Flies* using appropriate styles	Exploring the language of the novel
For coursework assessment of your contribution to a group discussion	For English Literature, section A	For English Literature, section A	For English Literature, section A

This unit has been written to help you to prepare for the final examination. It assumes that you have already been studying the text.

LITERATURE BASICS

What do you need to know for English Literature?

There are four assessment objectives:

The specification says . . .	So you need to . . .
1 respond to texts critically, sensitively, and in detail, selecting appropriate ways to convey your response, using textual evidence as appropriate	◆ know the texts really well ◆ learn about their content (what happens) and style (how they are written) ◆ know how to write about a text, including how to use quotations
2 explore how language, structure, and forms contribute to the meaning of texts, considering different approaches to texts and alternative interpretations	◆ be confident in discussing the language and structure of the text ◆ have ideas about different views of the text
3 explore relationships and comparisons within and between texts, selecting and evaluating relevant material	◆ make links between ideas in a text, and between the different texts you study ◆ support your points with examples
and in coursework: 4 relate texts to their social, cultural, and historical contexts and literary traditions	◆ know about other, earlier texts ◆ know about the context for this text – what the world was like when it was written

How many literature texts do I need to study for English Literature?

What do I need to study?	How will I be assessed?
Prose published before 1914	Coursework
Prose published after 1914 (eg *Lord of the Flies, Of Mice and Men, The Catcher in the Rye*)	Literature exam, section A
Poetry published before 1914 (anthology)	Literature exam, section B
Poetry published after 1914 (anthology)	Literature exam, section B
Drama published before 1914	Coursework (Shakespeare)
Drama written after 1914	Coursework

Do any of the coursework assignments also count for GCSE English?

Yes, Shakespeare and pre-1914 prose can count.

STUDYING PLOT

Remember:

To do well in English Literature you need to show understanding of many features. Just knowing the plot (storyline) is not enough to achieve a high grade. This section helps you to secure your knowledge of the plot so that you can then explore other features of the text.

Activity 1 Exploring the setting

1 Look at this description of the island in *Lord of the Flies*:

'It was roughly boat-shaped: humped near this end with behind them the jumbled descent to the shore. On either side rocks, cliffs, tree-tops, and a steep slope: forward there, the length of the boat, a tamer descent, tree-clad, with hints of pink: and then the jungly flat of the island, dense green, but drawn at the end to a pink tail. There, where the island petered out in water, was another island; a rock, almost detached, standing like a fort, facing them across the green with one bold, pink bastion.'

Sketch a map of the island. Use colours to reflect what William Golding says in his description.

2 Think about the following locations in *Lord of the Flies*.

27

For each one, say

- what happens there
- why it is an appropriate place for what happens
- why it is significant in the novel as a whole

Then put the places in order to show which you think is the most/least important setting.

- the beach
- the platform
- the mountain
- Castle Rock

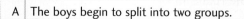

3 Look at these three photographs of beaches. If you were directing a new film of *Lord of the Flies*, which would you choose as the best location? Why?

Activity 2 The structure of the novel

1 Look at this list of events that happen in *Lord of the Flies*. Currently they are in the wrong order. Sort them out into the right order.

A	The boys begin to split into two groups.
B	Piggy and Ralph meet up after escaping from the shot-down plane.
C	Jack brings up hunting. Ralph says that keeping the fire going is much more important than hunting.
D	A man from a shot-down fighter plane parachutes down from the sky.
E	Piggy sees a conch shell, and shows Ralph how to use it to make a noise. Ralph uses it to call all of the other boys for a meeting.
F	There is a fight. Jack punches Piggy, breaking his glasses.
G	Ralph tries to escape from the advancing fire, making his way to Simon's den.
H	All the boys take part in a ritual dance. They attack 'the beast' which is actually Simon, whose body is carried by the current out to sea.
I	Jack's tribe begins to hunt, and they come across a sow and baby piglets. They attack and kill the mother sow. The head is put on a stick as a gift for the Beast.
J	At Castle Rock, Jack orders his tribe to grab Samneric, and tie them up.
K	Ralph suggests making a signal fire, so that they will get rescued. The boys go off to gather wood.
L	Jack's tribe are searching for fire. They steal Piggy's glasses.
M	A naval officer arrives to rescue the children. He says: 'Fun and games'.

2 Retell the story of *Lord of the Flies* in cartoon form using 8–12 frames. Aim it at someone younger than yourself who does not know the storyline. Try to tell the basic storyline as clearly as possible. Use labels to explain what happens in each frame.

Activity 3 Exploring the ending

At the end of the novel the naval officer says, 'I know. Jolly good show. Like the Coral Island.'

Why does Golding end the novel with this view?

Look at these two comments as a starting point, and then discuss your own interpretation.

Comment A
The naval officer's comment shows that everything can now be restored to normal. That's why Ralph cries – because he's pleased that things can be calm and pleasant again.

Comment B
The naval officer's comment shows how out-of-touch the adult world is. He thinks these are just a group of boys, rather than savages. The ending shows us how human beings misunderstand each other.

CHARACTERS

Activity 1 Exploring character

Working in pairs or small groups, choose one of the characters below and put together a spider diagram or poster.

Try to cover each of these headings. For each one, try to find an example or quotation from the text to support your point.

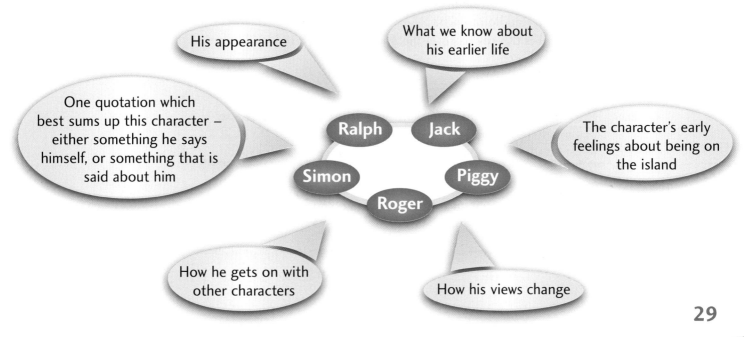

Then present your ideas to others in your class, and display the diagrams/posters.

Activity 2   Analysing characters

Look at the different scales. For each scale, decide where you would put each character. In a small group, and then as a class, discuss how you have reached your decision.

Characters:
*   Ralph
*   Jack
*   Simon
*   Piggy
*   Samneric

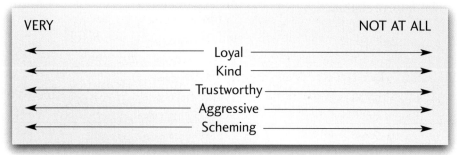

Activity 3   Character descriptions

Here are some quotations. Each one is about a different character in the novel. Which one belongs to which character … and how can you tell? See how many of the questions you can answer.

1   Which character?
*   Ralph
*   Jack
*   Simon
*   Piggy
*   Roger

2   How can you tell?
3   Which part of the novel do you think the quotation comes from (start, middle or end)?
4   What is the key word in the quotation which links it to that character?

A 'The boy who controlled them was dressed in the same way though his cap badge was golden.'

B 'There had grown up tacitly among the biguns the opinion that X was an outsider . . .'

C 'Only the beast lay still, a few yards from the sea. Even in the rain they could see how small a beast it was; and already its blood was staining the sand.'

D 'X stooped, picked up a stone, aimed, and threw it at Henry – threw it to miss . . . X's arm was conditioned by a civilisation that knew nothing of him and was in ruins.'

E 'He gave himself up to [the tears] now for the first time on the island; great, shuddering spasms of grief that seemed to wrench his whole body. His voice rose under the black smoke before the burning wreckage of the island; and infected by that emotion, the other little boys began to shake and sob too.'

Activity 4 Hot-seating

Working in small groups, hot-seat some of the characters in the novel. One of you should play the character; the others should think of questions which explore:

- the character's background
- his feelings towards other characters
- what goes through his mind at key moments
- his key ideas or preoccupations
- what he hopes will happen

Think about how you will phrase your questions to get high-level answers. Look at this example:

Low-level question	High-level question
Piggy, do you like Ralph?	Piggy, how do your views about Ralph develop during the novel?
This is a low-level question because it leads to a simple yes/no response	This is high-level because it allows the character's feelings to be explored in a lot of detail.

Spend some time thinking of appropriate questions for the different characters. You might include in the activity some of the minor characters, like Percival and Sam/Eric.

Activity 5 Focusing on Jack and Ralph

Although the reader's sympathies are usually with Ralph, many of the boys decide to follow Jack.

Why is this? Use drama techniques to hot-seat one of the boys. Draw up some questions, such as:

- ◆ What was your first impression of both Jack and Ralph?
- ◆ How did you feel as you listened to Ralph's ideas about keeping the fire going and working together?
- ◆ What do you like about Jack?
- ◆ Why did you decide to follow Jack?
- ◆ Have you at any point regretted that decision?

Activity 6 Writing about characters

Here are two extracts from students' assignments writing about the character of Ralph.

- ◆ What do you like in each example (look at the words the students use, the structure, the use of supporting evidence)?
- ◆ What do you think could be improved?
- ◆ What advice would you give to each student?

A: A character study of Ralph

Ralph is a nice person who tries to take control of things but he finds it very difficult because none of the boys will listen to him, except Piggy. Although Ralph likes Piggy he also gets annoyed by him and early on in the book he joins in when the other boys tease Piggy. This makes Ralph seem quite normal.

B: A character study of Ralph

At the start of the novel Ralph belongs between childhood and adolescence. The writer says: 'he was old enough, twelve years and a few months, to have lost the prominent tummy of childhood; and not yet old enough for adolescence to have made him awkward'. In some ways Ralph exists between two worlds. This is true throughout a lot of the novel. He is neither one of Jack's gang, not one of the littluns. He seems to be an outsider. He is also a natural leader. We can see this from the way he uses the conch to call a first meeting.

THEMES AND SYMBOLS

Activity 1 Exploring symbols

Writers use symbols to shape our feelings towards people and places. You need to be clear on the difference between signs and symbols:

Signs	Symbols
Have one meaning and are designed to inform us about something	Sum up a set of thoughts or ideas and may have a number of meanings
E.g. a red traffic light – means stop	E.g. a red poppy – symbolizes war, suffering, remembrance

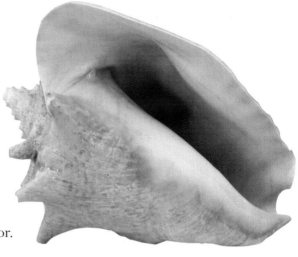

Here are some of the symbols in *Lord of the Flies*:

- conch
- beast
- pig's head
- fire
- masks/clothes
- glasses

1 Choose one or two of them and brainstorm their associations – things they might stand for. Think about how they might have different meanings for different people, or at different points in the story.
2 Present your ideas by quickly sketching the object and then labelling some of the different associations around it, like a spider diagram.
3 Look again at the list of symbols. Working in pairs, place them in order of most to least important in the novel. Compare your rank order with others in your class.

Activity 2 The symbol of the 'beast'

Simon says: 'Maybe there is a beast.'
Ralph says: 'But there isn't a beast.'
Jack says: 'We'll make sure when we go hunting.'

How does William Golding use the 'beast' in the novel as a whole?
Write a paragraph each about:
- what the 'beast' may symbolize
- how it is presented in the structure, language, and ideas of the novel
- the way the boys' ideas about the 'beast' change during the novel
- what effect the 'beast' has on different boys

Activity 3 Exploring themes

Themes are the issues that a text is about. For example, the theme of *Star Wars* might be good versus evil. *Lord of the Flies* has many themes. Look at the list below.

Working in pairs, choose **one** theme and brainstorm some examples of events that happen in the novel under that heading. To explore how the writer presents and develops his themes, try to group your points under a timeline like this:

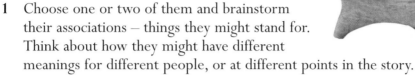

Initial crash ------ **Simon's death** ------ **Piggy's death** ------ **Rescue**

- civilization/savagery
- leadership
- good versus evil
- violence

- outsiders
- fear
- human nature

33

Activity 4 Responding to critics

Here are a number of comments on the novel's themes written by critics (people who read, comment on, and evaluate a text).

Read all of the critical comments. Put them in order to show which you most strongly agree with and which you disagree with.

For each comment, decide whether you:

Strongly agree ------   agree ------   disagree ------   strongly disagree

Discuss your reasons.

Civilization/savagery
The novel shows us that we are all savages underneath. Civilization soon breaks down and we see that without people in authority chaos rules.

Leadership
The novel shows us that some people are natural leaders and other people are followers. It also shows that to be a really successful leader you have to use brute force.

Good versus evil
The novel shows us that the world is an evil place. Good people, like Piggy and Simon, do not survive.

Violence
The novel shows that human beings always use violence to sort out their problems.

Outsiders
The novel shows us that people who are outsiders are often not accepted. There are many outsiders in the story (Piggy, Simon, Percival). All of them suffer for it.

Fear
The novel shows us that what we should be most fearful of is what is within us.

Human nature
The novel shows a completely negative view of human nature.

Activity 5 Writing about themes

Choose one of the themes and explore what we learn about it from the novel. Use these general prompts to get you started:

- How is the theme first presented?
- What different sides of the theme do we see?
- What do you think is the overall message or moral of the theme?

Activity 6 Exploring the title

Think about why the novel is called *Lord of the Flies*. Start by looking at these other possible titles:

- The Island
- Death's Day
- The Beast Within
- Choir Practice

1 Which of these titles do you think is suitable? Which are terrible? Would any of them work if the novel was re-presented as a major movie? Why?

In pairs or small groups, brainstorm any other titles you can think of.

2 Now think about Golding's title. Why do you think he calls the novel *Lord of the Flies*? Write down your explanation.

Activity 7 The 'grown ups'

At the end of Chapter 5, Ralph asks for 'something grown up . . . a sign or something'. What do you think is the significance of the 'world of grown ups' at this point in the story, and in the novel as a whole?

Think about:

- the different attitudes of the boys towards 'grown ups'
- events that occur on the island and in the outside world
- the writer's ideas and how he conveys them to the reader through language and structure

Activity 8 Discussion

What goes wrong on the island? If you were giving advice to the boys at the start on how to survive peacefully and successfully, what would you say? Discuss this in small groups, then report back to the class. Draw up a leaflet or poster containing **seven to ten** survival hints. They might focus on:

- how to behave
- how to organize
- how to get things done

Spot the Golding

A group of students were asked to write imitations of William Golding's style. This is the task they were given:

'A researcher has found William Golding's notebooks containing his earlier drafts of *Lord of the Flies*. Imagine they contain a forgotten extract from the book. What might it be like? Write one or two paragraphs from the forgotten text.'

Here are two responses. Which one feels closest to the style of *Lord of the Flies*? Using the prompts below, try to explain why.

Text A
The island sweltered under the punishing clouds. They forced the horizon ever downwards, as if trying to bury it beneath the shimmering blue of the sea. A noise in the undergrowth distracted Simon, and he turned to see a small, frightened piglet, not at all like the pink scrubbed creatures he half remembered from his days back home. It was dark and caked in something that might have been mud.

Text B
'I've got the conch,' shouted Piggy, and once the sneers died down, he looked around at the group of boys, their hair caked to their foreheads, their faces lined brown and white in lines of dirt and dribbling sweat. Piggy knew that this was his moment, his chance to have his say before the jeering started up again. 'The fire,' he said. 'Ralph's right, the fire's the most important thing'. Like dogs unleashed, the boys roared at him, roars of laughter and hatred, insults and jibes, and Piggy put down the conch, pushed it into the grey mass of sand at his feet, knowing, with eyes that began to prickle, that his chance was gone.

Compare the texts. You might focus on:

◆ use of description
◆ dialogue
◆ sensuous details (taste, smell, colours, and so on)
◆ choice of vocabulary
◆ length and type of sentences

Exploring descriptive writing
Look at this extract from the novel and then use the questions to explore the writer's style.

Simon looked up, feeling the weight of his wet hair, and gazed up at the sky. Up there, for once, were clouds, great bulging towers that sprouted away over the island, grey and cream and copper-coloured. The clouds were sitting on the land; they squeezed, produced moment by moment, this close, tormenting heat. Even the butterflies deserted the open space where the obscene thing grinned and dripped. Simon lowered his head, carefully keeping his eyes shut, then sheltered them with his hand. There were no shadows under the trees but everywhere a pearly stillness, so that what was real seemed illusive and without definition. The pile of guts was a black blob of flies that buzzed like a saw.

1 Golding makes his descriptions powerful by referring to various senses. Which of the five senses are described in this extract – sight, taste, touch, smell, sound?
2 How does Golding make nature seem menacing in this extract?
3 Look at the way Golding uses figurative language. For each example, say how the technique helps to describe the object.

Technique	Object described	The picture it creates
Simile (comparisons linked with *as* or *like*)	The pile of guts . . . buzzed like a saw	
Metaphor (comparing two objects without using *like* or *as*)	pearly stillness (saying the stillness was like a pearl)	
Personification (describing an object as if it is human)	The clouds were sitting on the land	
Personification	they squeezed, produced moment by moment, this close, tormenting heat	

SAMPLE EXAM QUESTIONS

1 How does Golding show that Ralph is changed by his experience on the island? What do you think he has learnt by the end?

You might focus on:

♦ what he is like when we first meet him
♦ how he responds to different events and situations
♦ how the writer presents the character of Ralph – for example, whether we find him a sympathetic (likeable) character
♦ Ralph's function in the novel – his importance and symbolic value
♦ your own opinions of Ralph

2 Write about **two** of the following themes as they are presented in the novel:

- violence and savagery
- children and adults
- loyalty and trust
- meetings and rituals

3 Ralph says, 'Things are breaking up. I don't understand why. We began well. We were happy.' Explain what goes wrong and why.

4 Write about the importance of the conch in *Lord of the Flies*, plus one of these other important items:

- Piggy's glasses
- the fire
- the parachutist
- the pig's head

5 How does William Golding show an increasing sense of violence in the novel? You might refer to:

- the events of the novel
- the behaviour of the characters
- how one act leads to another

WRITING ABOUT THE NOVEL

What does *Lord of the Flies* show us about human nature, and how does it show this?

Activity 1 Opening paragraphs

Compare these two opening paragraphs.

- Which do you think more successfully begins to address the question?
- Which words and phrases would you change?
- What advice would you give to the student?

Opening paragraph A

Throughout the novel William Golding explores human nature. It is revealed through Simon's conversation with the imaginary Lord of the Flies when he realizes that the real beast is one that exists in all the boys. We see it in 'the true, wise friend called Piggy', in the stone-throwing Roger, and in the gang-mentality which takes over the boys.

Opening paragraph B

William Golding wrote *Lord of the Flies* in 1954 and since then it has also been filmed several times. The novel and the films explore human nature. They show us its good sides as well as its bad sides. In this essay I will look at the ways in which the novel tells us about human nature.

Activity 2   Final paragraphs

Compare these two final paragraphs.

- Which do you think more successfully concludes the assignment?
- Which words and phrases would you change?
- What advice would you give to the student?

Final paragraph A

Lord of the Flies shows us many different views of human nature and it is neither all positive nor all negative. Piggy and Simon both show a feeling of goodness and caring for others. Roger and Jack show that humans can also be wicked. At the end Ralph cries, and this shows that he has learnt something. Therefore I think it is quite a positive ending.

Final paragraph B

Although Golding seems to present a bleak view of human nature, he does give the reader some hope for the future. At the end of the novel Ralph is a different boy and he 'weeps for the end of innocence'. He has seen and understood 'the darkness of man's heart' and has come to appreciate Piggy who earlier he had dismissed as a fool. The fact that he appears to have learnt something from his horrific experiences hints at a feeling of hope for the future. At least humans can learn from their mistakes.

SAMPLE ANSWER

Now look at this complete essay. Read the essay on the left-hand side of the page, keeping the Examiner's comments covered. See what you think are its strengths and weaknesses in:

- structure
- expression (words and sentences)
- style (e.g. use of quotations)

Then see what the examiner says.

Sample answer	Comments by Examiner
Throughout the novel William Golding explores human nature. It is revealed through Simon's conversation with the imaginary Lord of the Flies when he realizes that the real beast is one that exists in all the boys. We see it in 'the true, wise friend called Piggy', in the stone-throwing Roger, and in the gang-mentality which takes over the boys.	You start well. The opening shows clear engagement with the question and it is good that you include a quotation so early.
The boys start well, and this shows a positive side of human nature. They discover fire, they build shelters, and they explore the island. They each have different roles and, for a while, stick to them. Piggy, Ralph and Simon serve as reminders in the novel that there is lots to admire in humans. Each of them shows positive qualities of wisdom and goodness in their own way.	This is also a solid paragraph, but it risks being a bit general. It does need a quotation.
Piggy, for example, is intelligent and practical, despite his asthma and poor eyesight. In many ways he is the voice of science and reason on the island: 'Piggy, for all his ludicrous body, had brains'. Piggy first suggests that Ralph should 'find the others' and 'call a meeting'. He often comes up with the solutions to the boys' problems. He suggests putting the fire on the mountain.	Although very brief, this uses evidence well to highlight Piggy's character. You should include the concept of 'human nature' to show that you are addressing the question directly.
Golding presents Ralph as a natural leader and he tries to set up a form of democracy on the island – backed by the conch. He shows care for others and also displays courage when he volunteers to explore Castle Rock alone in search of the beast. He gets frustrated by others but never really loses his patience. At the end he has learnt about the 'darkness of man's heart' and understands too late the value of Piggy. Through Ralph, Golding shows us a positive side of human nature.	This shows a good insight into Ralph's character. You could show how his character develops – and how stable his nature is, despite being severely tested.
Jack is shown as someone who also has natural leadership but who exploits his power. At the start he is a dark figure on the beach, leading a 'creature' which proves to be the choirboys in procession. Jack is menacing from the start. He controls people through violence and he doesn't show the same sense of responsibility as Ralph – for example, letting the fire go out. He shows the weakness of human nature – the way we can be tempted to do things that are wrong. For example, using face-paints he loses his own identity and then starts to allow terrible things to happen, like the killing of Simon.	This paragraph is a bit generalized, with just one short quotation. The content is good, though it feels a bit rushed.

Sample answer	Comments by Examiner
The author also shows a positive side to human nature through Simon. At times he seems like a Christ-like figure and a saint. He more than anyone looks after the children – the littluns. He is tormented in the wilderness by the Beast (as Jesus was tempted by the Devil). He is finally tortured by people he should have been able to rely on. Simon is a true friend to Ralph – and encourages him to 'go on being Chief'. He seems mystical when he predicts that Ralph will 'get back all right'.	This explores Simon's character well, and it links well to the human nature theme.
Although Golding seems to present a depressing view of human nature, he does give the reader some hope for the future. At the end of the novel Ralph is a different boy and he 'weeps for the end of innocence'. He has seen and understood 'the darkness of man's heart' and has come to appreciate Piggy who earlier he had dismissed as a fool. The fact that he appears to have learnt something from his horrific experiences hints at a feeling of hope for the future. At least humans can learn from their mistakes.	This is a good conclusion, which draws the theme together well.

Conclusion

At times this reads a bit more like a character study than an exploration of human nature. You need to keep repeating the phrase 'human nature' in each paragraph to emphasize the theme. It is a bit odd starting with Piggy – you might have begun with Ralph first as the main character. Use of quotations is mostly good, though there is room for more. You need to say more about Golding's use of form, structure, and language. Your expression is mostly good, with some well-chosen, precise vocabulary. Overall – a very accomplished essay.

Work likely to be produced by a B+ grade candidate.

4 POST-1914 PROSE

JOHN STEINBECK, *Of Mice and Men*

In this unit you will develop these skills:

SPEAKING AND LISTENING	READING	WRITING	LANGUAGE WORKSHOP
Discussing different interpretations of the text	Reading *Of Mice and Men* to explore plot, character, themes, and language	Writing about *Of Mice and Men* using appropriate styles	Exploring the language of the novel
For coursework assessment of your contribution to a group discussion	For English Literature, section A	For English Literature, section A	For English Literature, section A

This unit has been written to help you to prepare for the final examination. It assumes that you have already been studying the text.

LITERATURE BASICS

What do you need to know for English Literature?

There are four assessment objectives:

The specification says . . .	So you need to . . .
1 respond to texts critically, sensitively, and in detail, selecting appropriate ways to convey your response, using textual evidence as appropriate	◆ know the texts really well ◆ learn about their content (what happens) and style (how they are written) ◆ know how to write about a text, including how to use quotations
2 explore how language, structure, and forms contribute to the meaning of texts, considering different approaches to texts and alternative interpretations	◆ be confident in discussing the language and structure of the text ◆ have ideas about different views of the text
3 explore relationships and comparisons within and between texts, selecting and evaluating relevant material	◆ make links between ideas in a text, and between the different texts you study ◆ support your points with examples
and in coursework: 4 relate texts to their social, cultural, and historical contexts and literary traditions	◆ know about other, earlier texts ◆ know about the context for this text – what the world was like when it was written

How many literature texts do I need to study for English Literature?

What do I need to study?	How will I be assessed?
Prose published before 1914	Coursework
Prose published after 1914 (eg *Lord of the Flies*, *Of Mice and Men*, *The Catcher in the Rye*)	Literature exam, section A
Poetry published before 1914 (anthology)	Literature exam, section B
Poetry published after 1914 (anthology)	Literature exam, section B
Drama published before 1914	Coursework (Shakespeare)
Drama written after 1914	Coursework

Do any of the coursework assignments also count for GCSE English?

Yes, Shakespeare and pre-1914 prose can count.

STUDYING CONTEXT

Set in 1930s California, *Of Mice and Men* shows a harsh environment. A series of droughts had led to crop failures. Whole families had to move, and many headed West in search of work. Those who managed to find work had to accept very bad working conditions and low pay, and many had to become migrant workers, moving from ranch to ranch in search of work. This is the life of Lennie Small and George Milton.

How important do you think it is to know about the historical context for the novel?

STUDYING PLOT

Activity 1 The structure of the novel

Look at this list of events mentioned in *Of Mice and Men*. Some of the events happen during the story. Some have happened before the story begins. Use the grid to:

1 sort them into the right order
2 decide which events are actually shown in the novel

	Event	Shown in the story . . . ?	. . . or referred to?
1	George shoots Lennie.		
2	Carlson shoots Candy's dog.		
3	George and Lennie hide in an irrigation ditch.		
4	Lennie talks to Crooks about the dream of a place of their own.		

	Event	Shown in the story . . . ?	. . . or referred to?
5	Lennie strokes Curley's wife's hair and finally kills her.		
6	George and Slim leave the ranch together.		
7	George tells Lennie to jump in the river. He does so. George saves his life and Lennie thanks him.		
8	George and Lennie arrive at the ranch.		
9	George and the other men go into town.		
10	Lennie runs and hides in the brush.		
11	The men play horseshoes.		
12	George and Lennie spend the night in the woods and George tells the story of their dream.		

3 Look at the events which are referred to rather than shown in the novel. Why do you think the writer chooses to tell us about the events in this way?

Activity 2 Examining the time-sequence

How clear are you about when events in the novel take place? They take place between Thursday night and Sunday afternoon. Try to match up the event to the correct time.

Look at the times below and match them up to the events listed.

Hot Thursday late afternoon	
Friday morning at the bunkhouse	
Friday evening	
Saturday night	
Sunday afternoon	
Sunday late afternoon	

a) Crook's room in the barn.

b) George and Lennie arrive at the ranch.

c) While the rest play horseshoes, Lennie kills his puppy in the barn.

d) Lennie's dead Aunt Clara appears and scolds him. Then George arrives.

e) Lennie gets a pup. Carlson shoots Candy's old dog with his Luger.

f) George and Lennie spend the night by the Salinas River.

Activity 3 Exploring the ending

Look again at the way the novel ends:

> Slim said: 'You hadda, George. I swear you hadda. Come on with me.' He led George into the entrance of the trail and up toward the highway.
> Curley and Carlson looked after them. And Carlson said: 'Now what the hell ya suppose is eatin' them two guys?'

A lot of readers feel disappointed when they first read the ending of the novel. Here are the comments of some Year 11 students:

- ◆ 'The first time I read the ending I thought there was a page missing.'
- ◆ 'It's too sudden. It doesn't make sense.'
- ◆ 'I like the ending now, but the first time I read the book it seemed a bit of a let-down.'

Imagine you are John Steinbeck. Write a paragraph explaining why you finished the novel in the way that you did. What were you trying to show by:

- ◆ Slim and George leaving the ranch together
- ◆ not explaining where they were going or why they were leaving
- ◆ giving Carlson the last word
- ◆ not telling us what happened next?

Explain the hints you had given earlier in the novel.

Activity 4 New endings

Imagine a Hollywood producer is about to make a new film version of *Of Mice and Men*. He wants a more satisfying ending. How might the novel have ended differently?

Here are some possible ideas for endings. Do any of them seem possible, or are they all too far-fetched?

For each one discuss why it is/is not a good possible ending. Write down your conclusions.

You might start your comment like this:

This is/is not a good ending because . . .

 Ending 1: Slim and George go into town, drink heavily, return to the ranch, get fired, and leave to find new jobs.

Ending 2: Curley regrets his behaviour and apologizes to George for all that has happened. He gives him money towards getting a place of his own.

45

Ending 3: Slim and George sit in a bar discussing Lennie. They decide that it's important to keep the dream alive and will keep working at the farm until they can raise enough money to buy a place of their own.

Activity 5 Suspense in the story

Discuss how John Steinbeck creates a drama in Carlson shooting Candy's old dog. How does he build suspense at this stage of the story?

EXPLORING THE SETTING

Activity 1 Exploring place

Look at this map of northern California. The arrows highlight four key references in the novel. For each one, say what happens at that place, or why it is mentioned in the novel.

Weed

Sacramento

San Francisco

Oakland

San José

Salinas

Salinas River

Gabilan mountains

SIERRA NEVADA

GABILAN MTS.

Activity 2 Imagining the ranch

Look at the different pictures of ranches on the previous page. Which one is closest to the way you visualize the ranch in *Of Mice and Men*? Which is least like your mental image?

Try to describe exactly why each image is/is not as you imagine the ranch in the novel.

Activity 3 Exploring nature

The novel starts and ends with a scene of nature.

Beginning of the first chapter:
A few miles south of Soledad, the Salinas River drops in close to the hill-side bank and runs deep and green.

Beginning of the last chapter:
The deep green pool of the Salinas River was still in the late afternoon.

◆ Why do you think the novel starts and ends in a natural setting, rather than at the ranch?
◆ Why is Lennie associated with nature?

CHARACTERS

Activity 1 Who said what?

Here are some quotations from *Of Mice and Men*. Identify who said which one . . . and to whom.

a) 'I could pet it with my thumb while we walked along.'
b) 'Guys like us, that work on ranches are the loneliest guys in the world . . . They don't belong no place.'
c) 'Guy don't need no sense to be a nice fella. Seems to me sometimes it jus' works the other way around. Take a real smart guy and he ain't hardly ever a nice fella.'
d) 'S'pose I went in with you guys . . . I could cook and tend the chickens and hoe the garden some. How'd that be?'
e) 'You guys travel around together?'

Activity 2 Comparing characters

What do we learn in the novel about different characters? Use a grid like the one on the next page to draw together your ideas, then write a paragraph about each.

Character	Physical appearance	Behaviour	Personality
Lennie			
George			
Slim			
Candy			
Curley's wife			

Activity 3 George

1   George sometimes expresses his frustration about being with Lennie. For example, he says: 'If I was alone, I could live so easy'. Yet he looks after Lennie all the time.

The Boss says: 'I never seen one guy take so much trouble for another guy. I just like to know what your interest is'.

Here are some possible reasons that George looks after Lennie. Put the statements in order from the one you MOST agree with to the LEAST:

a)   He feels that he must look after Lennie because he promised Aunt Clara (duty).
b)   He likes Lennie.
c)   He feels sorry for Lennie.
d)   He wouldn't know how to cope without Lennie.
e)   Lennie gives a purpose to his life.

2   What do you think George would do without Lennie? How would his life be different? In a group brainstorm:

◆   What kind of job would George do if he hadn't met Lennie?
◆   How would his life be different?

3   George is usually described positively by most readers. But look at what this student says:

'I don't like George. He looks after Lennie but he treats him badly. He is always putting him down. Although he keeps talking about their dream, he selfishly goes to Susy's place (a brothel), wasting their money.'

How far do you agree with this? Why? What evidence would you use?

Activity 4 Lennie

1   Lennie has strengths and weaknesses. For example, he is very trusting (a strength) but very forgetful (a weakness). Use a table like this to brainstorm his other strengths and weaknesses.

Strengths	Weaknesses

Look at your list. Which is the MAIN strength and MAIN weakness?

2 What does Lennie like about George and what does he dislike? Working in twos or threes, hot-seat Lennie, asking him questions about the things he likes about George (for example, that George helps him) and the things he dislikes (for example, George takes the mouse away).

3 Working in pairs, find quotations which sum up Lennie. Aim to find five quotations about him. Find another five things he himself says which you think are important or typical.

Activity 5 Exploring the minor characters

On the ranch there are several minor characters who play an important part in the story. Explore their role in the following sequence of activities:

1 Candy says about Curley:

'Curley's like a lot of little guys. He hates big guys. He's alla time picking scraps with big guys. Kind of like he's mad at 'em because he ain't a big guy.'

- Is there anything at all we can like about Curley, or is he simply a bully?
- Does John Steinbeck hint at any weaknesses or flaws that might make us warm to his character?
- How do you explain his reasons for marrying?

2 Curley is quoted as saying that he's keeping his hand soft for his wife. George replies: 'That's a dirty thing to tell around'. Later he says: 'I bet he's eatin' raw eggs and writin' to the patent medicine houses'. What does George mean by this?

3 Many of the characters in *Of Mice and Men* are basically lonely. Working in pairs, look at the list below and decide who you think is most/least lonely and how you can tell.

- George
- Candy
- Curley's wife

4 How does Candy feel over the shooting of the dog? Why is he so passive? What does he mean later when he says: 'I ought to of shot that dog myself, George'?

Write a one-paragraph diary entry for that evening in which he explains how he feels.

You might start like this:

This has been one of the worst days of my life . . .

Activity 6 Curley's wife

1 We never learn the name of Curley's wife. Why do you think this is?

2 Curley's wife used to have glamorous ambitions. She dreamt of being an actress. Re-read the section where she talks to Lennie about her dreams. Then write a paragraph from her diary in which she describes the night she first met Curley. You might start like this:

Today I think the dream may be about to begin. I met a man today who . . .

3 Explore the way different characters talk about and behave towards Curley's wife.

- Lennie
- George
- Slim
- Curley
- Crooks

You might use words like:

- contemptuous (treating her as if she is inferior)
- wary (being cautious of her)
- attracted to her
- kind
- neutral
- fearful

Present your ideas as a spider diagram with Curley's wife at the centre. Write down the other characters' names around her and a word to describe their attitude towards her. Where possible, find a quotation from the novel that supports your view.

4 Look at this description of Curley's wife:

> 'A girl was standing there looking in. She had full, rouged lips and wide-spaced eyes, heavily made up. Her finger-nails were red. Her hair hung in little rolled clusters, like sausages. She wore a cotton house dress and red mules, on the insteps of which were little bouquets of red ostrich feathers.'

- Comment on the underlined words and phrases.
- Comment on the use of colour in the extract.
- Why do you think John Steinbeck describes her hair using a simile about sausages?
- What overall impression of Curley's wife does this extract create?

5 Some readers react strongly against Curley's wife. Like George they see how dangerous she is. Others feel sympathy for her, locked in a loveless marriage.

Using a table like this, make notes on ways we might feel sympathetic or unsympathetic for her:

Sympathetic features (i.e. reasons we might like her or feel sorry for her)	Unsympathetic features (i.e. reasons for not liking her, or not feeling sorry for her)

What is your overall response to Curley's wife?

THEMES AND SYMBOLS

Activity 1 Exploring the title

The novel gets its name from some lines in a poem by the Scottish poet, Robert Burns, called 'To a Mouse':

The best-laid schemes o' mice an' men
Gang aft a-gley

- See if you can work out what the quotation means.
- Then think about why it is relevant to the novel.

Activity 2 Responding to critics

One critic writing about *Of Mice and Men* says:

'There are references to Arthurian legend in the novel. George moves around the ranch like Sir Galahad (a hero of old English legends). He protects Lennie, and their journey towards a ranch of their own is a kind of quest.'

In pairs or small groups, discuss how far you agree with this statement.

Activity 3 Symbolic events

One of the reasons *Of Mice and Men* is so powerful is that John Steinbeck hints at what is to happen. For example, look at these hints:

- In Weed, Lennie touches the girl's red dress
- The pet mouse is killed by Lennie
- Candy's dog is shot by Carlson
- The puppy is killed by Lennie

How do these events hint at what will happen next?
What other hints are there in the novel?

LANGUAGE WORKSHOP

1 John Steinbeck uses dialect words to show the way the characters speak. How does the dialect differ from standard English?

a) Use a grid like the one below to explore some of the differences.

American dialect	Standard English
Them guys just come	
We hadda walk ten miles	
So you wasn't gonna say a word	
We was diggin' a cesspool	
You let Curley take the rap	
This ain't no good place	
I never done nothing, George	

b) If the dialogue was written in standard English, would it work? What would the reader lose?

2 Look at the way John Steinbeck uses speech verbs during dialogue.

Some writers use various synonyms (similar words) to avoid repeating the verb *said*. In general John Steinbeck is happy to keep using *said*. Sometimes he uses other speech verbs (such as *replied*).

Take a sample of two pages and look at the way he uses dialogue. Use a table like this one to catalogue the way he organizes characters' speech. Then use your data to answer the questions below.

Chosen pages: ____		
Number of times he uses *said*	Number of times he uses no speech verb at all	Other speech verbs used (write down how often for each one)

a) Look at your data. What is the most frequent way that John Steinbeck tells us who has said something?
b) What percentage of his dialogue uses the speech verb said?
c) What percentage uses no speech verb?
d) What is the effect of these choices?

SAMPLE EXAM QUESTIONS

1 *Of Mice and Men* ends where it begins, with George and Lennie, alone by the pool.

What is your response to the ending of the novel?

Write about:

- your feelings about George's decision to shoot Lennie
- ways in which Steinbeck prepares us for this ending
- why the writer chooses to end the story in this way
- whether the ending suggests that the friendship between George and Lennie was pointless.

2 Write about the importance of the different places in *Of Mice and Men*, real or imagined.

3 Show how John Steinbeck explores the complex relationship between George and Lennie.

You should write about:

- what keeps them together, and the difficulties they each have
- how the writer brings out differences between them
- how they are different from other people on the farm
- what you think Steinbeck's purpose was in writing about this relationship.

4 Hopes and dreams help people to survive, even if they can never become real. How true is this for characters in *Of Mice and Men*?

5 How does Steinbeck create a sense of insecurity in the novel?

You should write about:

- why some characters may feel insecure
- uses of language
- the contribution of the settings
- other features which create a sense of insecurity.

6 The following passage is taken from near the beginning of Chapter 4 where Crooks is talking to Lennie.

How does Steinbeck present Crooks in this passage? What is the importance of Crooks in the novel as a whole?

'But I know now.' He hesitated, and when he spoke again his voice was softer: 'There wasn't another coloured family for miles around. And now there ain't a coloured man on this ranch an' there's jus' one family in Soledad.' He laughed. 'If I say something, why it's just a nigger sayin' it.'

Lennie asked, 'How long you think it'll be before them pups will be old enough to pet?'

Crooks laughed again. 'A guy can talk to you an' be sure you won't go blabbin'. Couple of weeks an' them pups'll be all right. George knows what he's about. Jus' talks, an' you don't understand nothing.' He leaned forward excitedly. 'This is just a nigger talkin', an' a busted-back nigger. So it don't mean nothing, see? You couldn't remember it anyways. I seen it over an' over an' over – a guy talkin' to another guy and it don't make no difference if he don't hear or understand. The thing is, they're talkin', or they're settin' still not talkin'. It don't make no difference, no difference.' His excitement had increased until he pounded his knee with his hand. 'George can tell you screwy things, and it don't matter. It's just the talking. It's just bein' with another guy. That's all.' He paused.

His voice grew soft and persuasive. 'S'pose George don't come back no more. S'pose he took a powder and just ain't coming back. What'll you do then?'

Lennie's attention came gradually to what had been said. 'What?' he demanded.

'I said s'pose George went into town to-night and you never heard of him no more.' Crooks pressed forward some kind of private victory. 'Just s'pose that,' he repeated.

'He won't do it,' Lennie cried. 'George wouldn't do nothing like that. I been with George a long time. He'll come back to-night ...' But the doubt was too much for him. 'Don't you think he will?'

Crooks' face lighted with pleasure in his torture.

7 *Of Mice and Men* shows us that people can be cruel, or kind, or sometimes a mixture of both. Compare three characters.

Write about:

◆ the ways in which the different characters are cruel, or kind, or a mixture of both
◆ why they behave as they do
◆ how you respond to them
◆ how Steinbeck writes about them to make you respond this way.

8 Remind yourself of the description of Lennie's fight with Curley in Chapter 3.

Write about the importance of this passage in *Of Mice and Men*.

Write about:

◆ the different aspects of Lennie shown in the passage
◆ what is revealed about the relationship between George and Lennie, and about Curley
◆ how this passage links with other parts of the novel
◆ the importance of the passage in the novel as a whole.

9 Many characters in *Of Mice and Men* are shown to be lonely.

Write about loneliness in the novel.

You should write about:

◆ characters who are lonely
◆ how the writer shows their loneliness
◆ the differences and similarities between lonely characters
◆ what you think the writer is saying about loneliness.

10 Find the passage in the novel where Lennie kills Curley's wife, from the description of the barn to the point when Lennie leaves to go to the brush.

Write about:

◆ why the writer begins this passage with the dead puppy
◆ why Lennie and Curley's wife behave in the way they do
◆ how the writer makes the death seem unavoidable
◆ whether you were surprised when you first read about her death, and why.

11 In Chapter 2 the ranch boss says to George:

'What's your stake in this guy? . . . I never seen one guy take so much trouble for another guy.'

Write about the relationship between George and Lennie. What is it that holds them together, and why does George decide to kill Lennie?

You should write about:

♦ their hopes, fears, and dreams
♦ the kind of relationship they have, and what it gives to each of them
♦ how the writer brings out the differences between them
♦ why the writer chooses to end the novel with George killing Lennie.

WRITING ABOUT THE NOVEL

Activity 1 Opening paragraphs

Look more closely at this question.

Many characters in *Of Mice and Men* are shown to be lonely. Write about loneliness in the novel.

♦ How would you approach this question?
♦ How would you plan an answer?
♦ What would you say in your first paragraph?

Now read these two opening paragraphs from student answers to this question.

Decide:

♦ what you think are the strengths and weaknesses of each paragraph
♦ which is the better paragraph overall.

You might think about:

♦ how well they begin to answer the question
♦ the style they use
♦ their use of examples and quotations.

Paragraph A

Loneliness is an important theme in the book. Many characters feel lonely and I am going to show who they are and why they feel lonely. The first character who feels lonely is Curley's wife. That is one reason that she hangs around the men on the ranch so much. She isn't really a flirt, but she is desperate for company.

Paragraph B

Many characters in the novel feel a sense of loneliness. This includes both the major and minor characters. George's relationship with Lennie is an unusual one because they seem so mismatched. After Lennie's death, George heads down the road with Slim. 'Now what the hell ya suppose is eatin' them two guys?' says Carlson. This is a hint that George needs companionship and is desperate not to be lonely.

Activity 2   Final paragraphs

Look at this question:

Hopes and dreams help people to survive, even if they can never become real.
How true is this for characters in *Of Mice and Men*?

Now look at the final paragraphs of two essays answering this question.

Think about:

- what you would expect in a good conclusion to a question like this
- how each student has brought the themes together
- which is the more successful conclusion.

Paragraph C

'I bet we could swing her,' says George. 'His eyes were full of wonder'. It seems as if his and Lennie's dream of owning a place of their own might finally be about to come true. He is just one character in the novel who is motivated by a desire to make something more of his life, just as Curley's wife believes she could still be a Hollywood actress. *Of Mice and Men* shows various characters' dreams. It also shows how fragile those dreams are, and how unlikely anyone is to achieve them.

Paragraph D

Hopes and dreams are very important in life. *Of Mice and Men* shows us various characters who have hopes and dreams – including Lennie, George, Curley's wife, Candy, and Crooks. Many of them are attracted to Lennie and George's dreams and this helps them to survive.

SAMPLE ANSWER 1

Read this sample answer written by a Year 11 student. The question is: 'Describe the importance of dreams to different characters.' Cover up the Examiner's comments and make up your own mind about its strengths and weaknesses. Then compare your views with the Examiner's.

Sample answer	Comments by Examiner
Dreams are very important in *Of Mice and Men*. George and Lennie's dream is to 'live off the fatta the lan'. This means that they dream to buy their own land and be their own boss and work there every day. They also want to be fed from there and Lennie wants to 'tend' his rabbits. Lennie makes the mistake of telling people about the dream and then they want to be part of it too. As soon as Candy finds out that George and Lennie have a dream, Candy offers all his savings. George gets really cross when he learns that Lennie has been talking about it, but he is also pleased that the dream may happen a bit sooner because of the money. He says: 'I bet we could swing her'. This means he thinks they could get the place.	The first sentence is good. It leads straight into the topic. The rest of the paragraph is too long, and it re-tells the story too much. It has a quotation early on but needs more references like this to the novel.
George and Lennie's 'dream farm' is a version of the American dream. This is the dream of being successful and being your own boss. It is an escape from the poverty and horrible life they have to lead. It means being in control of your own life. George says: 'I'll take my fifty bucks an' I'll stay all night in some lousy cat house. Or I'll set in some pool-room till ever' body goes home.'	This is a fair point but a bit general. The word *horrible* is too babyish for an essay like this. You should find a better word, such as *squalid/grim/ unfulfilling/depressing/dismal.*
Curley's wife has a dream too. She dreams of being a famous actress and she thought at first that different men would help her to achieve this dream. She says: 'I met a guy, an' he was in pitchers. Went out to the Riverside Dance Palace with him. He says he was gonna put me in the movies. Says I was a natural.'	Curley's wife is a good choice of character. You could say more about exactly what her dreams were and the fact that she still thinks she might achieve them.
She puts a lot of trust in men and is always let down by them: 'I never got that letter'.	This doesn't need to be a separate paragraph.
She is someone who has a strong dream but it has crumbled so when she hears about Lennie and George's dream she becomes interested and this makes her start to think about her own dreams again. She trusts Lennie and confides in him.	Again, this should follow on as part of the previous paragraph.
Other characters don't really have dreams so when they hear about what Lennie and George are planning they become interested and want to take part. Crooks for example sees it as a way of being badly treated and escaping from a life as a servant.	The essay feels rushed here. There is more to say about the way Crooks wants to escape from his current situation.
But because they tell their dream to other people it falls apart.	This is a very abrupt (sudden) ending. In general concluding paragraphs need to draw ideas together better than this.

Conclusion

This answer is very brief. The main problems are that it lacks a clear structure and is short of supporting examples. It does however show some understanding of the characters.

Work likely to be produced by a C- grade candidate.

SAMPLE ANSWER 2

The response below is to the following question: 'Look at the opening of the scene in which Lennie is alone in Crooks' room. How does the scene increase our understanding of both Lennie and Crooks?'

Sample answer	Comments by Examiner
This extract gives a detailed description of Crooks, his room, and his possessions. It shows the effect Lennie has on Crooks during his visit. At the beginning of the extract Lennie is not welcomed into Crooks' room, but by the end they have begun to understand and perhaps trust each other. It is another example of the way Lennie makes people trust him and start to talk openly about personal feelings. Curley's wife also does this, and so does George.	This starts very well. It has a clear focus on the early part of the scene. It needs a quotation or two.
Crooks' room tells us about the sad life he leads. He has few possessions. There is 'a mauled copy of the California civil code for 1905' and some 'gold-rimmed spectacles'. These suggest that he is educated and aware of his rights, even though he is treated in a cruel way. He is a victim of prejudice. The book shows that he is aware of this. Despite the way he is treated 'Crooks was a proud, aloof man'. John Steinbeck helps us to feel sympathy for him, whilst also showing that Crooks is self-contained and able to rely on himself.	There is some good detail here, well supported by quotations. The point about Crooks' possessions, and what these reveal about him, is good.
It becomes clear in this scene that he has suffered years of loneliness. He is very annoyed when Lennie first enters the room, saying 'You got no right to come in my room. This here's my room'. Crooks is protective of his own territory and – after years of being abused – distrusts anyone who approaches him. We can see how proud he is from the way he is eager to show that he is a good worker. He tries to reassure Lennie that he can still work hard despite his disability. He wants to join George and Lennie's dream to give his life more purpose. This is emphasised by the fact that he is willing to work for just a bed and some food and go without wages.	This paragraph also contains good points. It needs some more supporting quotations.
The men on the ranch are pleasant to Crooks only when it suits them. For example, at Christmas 'they let the nigger come in'. Lennie however treats him as an equal and simply wants someone to talk to. At times Crooks talks cruelly about this, taunting Lennie about George not coming back. This gets Lennie upset and 'Crooks saw the danger as it approached him'. This shows a cruel streak in Crooks, but it is probably because he is jealous of Lennie having someone who he can trust. Lennie certainly trusts George totally, saying 'He'll come back to-night'.	This paragraph isn't directly relevant to the question. It is about the way the other characters treat Crooks rather than about his relationship with Lennie in a single scene.
Lennie's language is simpler than Crooks'. This is because Crooks is educated and Lennie is not and is mentally below average. The scene shows that although the two characters do not have much in common they learn a lot from each other, and we learn a lot from seeing them in this scene.	This promises to focus on the language but it actually says little. It does draw together a few of the themes of the essay as a whole.

Conclusion

This answer starts well. It lacks a clear structure and doesn't have enough supporting points. For a top grade it needs to say more about the language used in the novel.

Work likely to be produced by a B grade candidate.

5 POST-1914 PROSE

J.D. SALINGER, *The Catcher in the Rye*

In this unit you will develop these skills:

SPEAKING AND LISTENING	READING	WRITING	LANGUAGE WORKSHOP
Discussing different interpretations of the text	Reading *The Catcher in the Rye* to explore plot, character, themes, and language	Writing about *The Catcher in the Rye* using appropriate styles	Exploring the language of the novel
For coursework assessment of your contribution to a group discussion	For English Literature, section A	For English Literature, section A	For English Literature, section A

This unit has been written to help you to prepare for the final examination. It assumes that you have already been studying the text.

LITERATURE BASICS

What do you need to know for English Literature?

There are four assessment objectives:

The specification says . . .	So you need to . . .
1 respond to texts critically, sensitively, and in detail, selecting appropriate ways to convey your response, using textual evidence as appropriate	◆ know the texts really well ◆ learn about their content (what happens) and style (how they are written) ◆ know how to write about a text, including how to use quotations
2 explore how language, structure, and forms contribute to the meaning of texts, considering different approaches to texts and alternative interpretations	◆ be confident in discussing the language and structure of the text ◆ have ideas about different views of the text
3 explore relationships and comparisons within and between texts, selecting and evaluating relevant material	◆ make links between ideas in a text, and between the different texts you study ◆ support your points with examples
and in coursework: 4 relate texts to their social, cultural, and historical contexts and literary traditions	◆ know about other, earlier texts ◆ know about the context for this text — what the world was like when it was written

How many literature texts do I need to study for English Literature?

What do I need to study?	How will I be assessed?
Prose published before 1914	Coursework
Prose published after 1914 (eg *Lord of the Flies, Of Mice and Men, The Catcher in the Rye*)	Literature exam, section A
Poetry published before 1914 (anthology)	Literature exam, section B
Poetry published after 1914 (anthology)	Literature exam, section B
Drama published before 1914	Coursework (Shakespeare)
Drama written after 1914	Coursework

Do any of the coursework assignments also count for GCSE English?

Yes, Shakespeare and pre-1914 prose can count.

STUDYING CONTEXT

Activity 1   The early 1950s

The Catcher in the Rye was published in 1951. To help you to imagine the what life was like at that time, here are some key historical facts and images:

Humphrey Bogart in The African Queen

The opening of Guys and Dolls

The United Nations building in New York

1950

- famous writers: Ray Bradbury, Ernest Hemingway, Tennessee Williams
- musical comedy, New York: *Guys and Dolls*
- 'cool' jazz music develops
- United Nations building, New York opened
- antihistamines become a popular remedy for cold and flu
- London population 8.3 million; New York 7.8 million
- 1.5 million TV sets in the USA

1951

- famous painters: Salvador Dali, Picasso, Matisse
- films of the year: *The African Queen, An American in Paris, Strangers on a Train*
- popular songs: 'Hello Young Lovers', 'In the Cool, Cool, Cool of the Evening'
- first solo flight over the North Pole
- colour TV introduced in USA

Based on your reading of the novel, brainstorm a list of other clues in the book about the time when it was set. Put together a poster which shows the context for the book. Or you might imagine that you are producing a poster for a film version of the novel, and think about the images you would use to conjure up the mood and background of the period.

Activity 2   Shock value

Many readers of *The Catcher in the Rye* were shocked when the novel was published. Re-read this opening sentence:

> *If you really want to hear about it, the first thing you'll probably want to know is where I was born, and what my lousy childhood was like, and how my parents were occupied and all before they had me, and all that David Copperfield kind of crap, but I don't feel like going into it . . .*

Which of these reasons might best explain why some people were shocked:

a) It is a confusing opening because we don't know who is speaking.
b) The narrator uses bad language.
c) The style feels like spoken rather than written English.
d) It feels as if the narrator is speaking to us directly.
e) The style feels negative and pessimistic.

Activity 3   Presenting the novel

The writer J. D. Salinger is very secretive and has strong views. For example, he refuses to give interviews and does not grant permission for people to use substantial extracts of the novel in other books (like this one). He also insists that the covers of all his novels are plain.

1   Look at the packaging of *The Catcher in the Rye*. If you were re-designing the cover for a modern audience, what would it be like? Would you use:

◆   an image – photographic/art?
◆   a particular style for the title and author's name
◆   a quotation about the book (e.g. 'An undoubted classic' – A. Forgham, *Books Today*)

Sketch what your cover might look like, and then write a short paragraph explaining the choices you have made. Use a style like this:

I used a photographic image of a 16-year-old boy because . . .
I chose to keep the photograph in black and white because . . .

2   Some readers like the plain packaging of the novel. They say it focuses them on what the story is about rather than on the designer's images. Do you agree? Should this apply to all novels, packaging them much more simply?

Activity 4   Reacting to the novel

Here are some comments made by critics and reviewers when *The Catcher in the Rye* was first published.

David Stevenson	Salinger 'gives us a chance to catch quick, half-amused, half-frightened glimpses of ourselves and our contemporaries, as he confronts us with his brilliant mirror images'
Charles Kegle	'His problem is one of communication: as a teenager, he simply cannot get through to the adult world which surrounds him; as a sensitive teenager, he cannot get through to others of his own age'
Robert Coles	Salinger is 'an original and gifted writer, a marvellous entertainer, a man free of the slogans and clichés the rest of us fall prey to'
Anne Goodman	'Holden was not quite so sensitive and perceptive as he, and his creator, thought he was . . . *The Catcher in the Rye* is a brilliant *tour de force*, but in a writer of Salinger's undeniable talent one expects something more'
James Stern	'That's the way it sounds to me, Hel said (a friend of the author), and away she went with this crazy book, *The Catcher in the Rye*. What did I tell ya, she said the next day. This Salinger, he's a short story guy. And he knows how to write about kids. This book, though, it's too long. Gets kinds of monotonous. And he should have cut out a lot about these jerks and all at that crumby school. They depress me. They really do. Salinger, he's best with real children. I mean the ones like Phoebe, his kid sister. She's a personality. Holden and little Phoebe, Hel said, they kill me. This last part about her and this Mr Antolini, the only guy Holden ever thought he could trust, who ever took any interest in him, and who turned out queer – that's terrific. I swear it is'
Paul Engle	The story was 'emotional without being sentimental, dramatic without being melodramatic, and honest without simply being obscene . . . The story is engaging and believable . . . full of right observations and sharp insight, and a wonderful sort of grasp of how a boy can create his own world of fantasy and live forms.'

Decide:

- what each critic is saying about the novel
- which ones are referring to the **content** (what the novel is about)
- which are referring to **style** (the way the novel is written)
- which comments you agree/disagree with

Activity 5   Writing a review

Imagine you are reviewing the novel for the first time. What would you say about it? Read the following advice for reviewers, and then write your own review.

Content advice

There are usually two elements in a good review:

1   Telling us what the play/film is about or what the song/product is like
2   Giving an opinion about how good it is

Element 1 is usually more factual: 'This is the latest novel by . . . It shows a change in style since her last . . .'

Element 2 is usually more opinion-based: 'This is far less entertaining than X's last novel. Although the storyline has odd moments of suspense, too much of it simply creaks along. I kept expecting a surprise twist at the end. The only surprise was that there wasn't a surprise. Overall, the novel is a serious disappointment.'

Style advice

Reviews are a chance to give your opinion – but you do not need to use *I* or *me* all the time. It's just as effective to say 'The novel has a powerful sense of place' as 'I think the novel has a powerful sense of place . . .'

Be creative – aim to make your review lively and entertaining. Write the kind of review you would like to read.

In evaluating the novel (i.e. giving your opinion), try to avoid using predictable evaluative words like *good* or *bad*. Here are some suggestions:

Some synonyms for *good*	lively enjoyable tense taut fascinating powerful evocative memorable amusing comic hilarious well-structured precise gripping enlightening entertaining convincing
Some synonyms for *bad*	dull tedious uninteresting uninspiring deadly banal unrealistic unconvincing depressing clichéd slack unstructured rambling

STUDYING PLOT

Activity 1   The events of the novel

Look at this summary of the novel. It is currently in the wrong order.
- Place it in the right order.
- What were the main clues that helped you to sort it out?

A	Depressed, Holden turns to the only person he can relate to, his sister Phoebe. He sneaks into his parent's apartment at night to talk to his sister. He tells her about his dream to be a 'catcher in the rye', and that he wants to run away.
B	One Saturday night, after a series of bad experiences at school, Holden decides to leave Pencey four days early for Christmas break.
C	Holden spends the next three days wandering aimlessly around New York City.
D	Holden ends up in a mental hospital for treatment.
E	Holden is unhappy at school and cannot relate to anyone (except for his kid sister Phoebe, everyone else seems to him a 'phoney').
F	The next day, he talks with some nuns about literature and has a date with his former girlfriend Sally Woodruff.
G	Holden Caulfield is a seventeen-year-old boy from New York City, telling the story of three days in his life.
H	Finally, he meets his sister, who says she wants to run away with him and that she will never go back to school.
I	He stays at a cheap hotel for one night.
J	He then leaves to meet his former teacher, Mr Antolini. They have a good talk, but Holden leaves when he thinks his host makes sexual advances towards him. He spends the night in a train station, then runs around town.

Activity 2   Examining the time-sequence

The events of the novel take place over just three days:
Saturday's events – chapters 1–14
Sunday's events – chapters 15–24
Monday's events – chapters 25–26

They also take place in various locations in Pennsylvania (at school) and in New York City.

Look at the list of locations on the next page. For each one, say what happens there and say which day the events take place on.

Location	Events	Day
Mr Spencer's room at school (chapter 2)		
Holden leaves school (end of chapter 7)		
Arrival in Penn Station (chapter 9)		
Museum of Natural History (end of chapter 16)		
The Wicker Bar (chapter 19)		
In the dark in Central Park (chapter 20)		
The Zoo (end of chapter 25)		

Activity 3 Examining the locations

Now do the same kind of activity using this map of New York. The arrows highlight some of the main locations used in the novel. Work out what happens at each location.

Then number the arrows to show the order the events take place in (so if the zoo is the first location that occurs in the novel, put a number one by it . . . and so on).

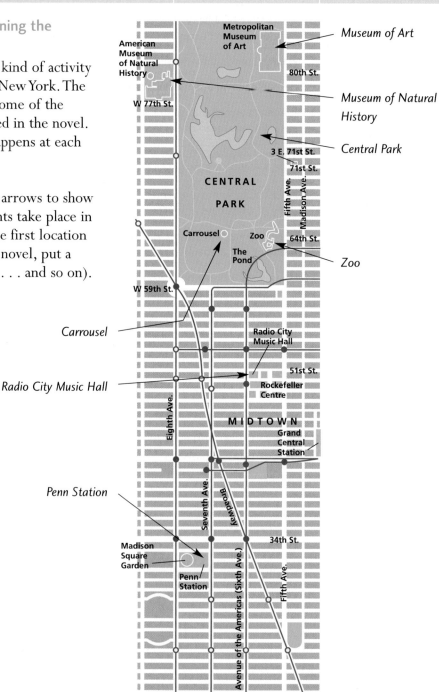

EXPLORING THE ENDING

Activity 1 Critics' views

Critics have different views of the ending of the novel. They sometimes imagine what will happen to Holden after the story finishes.

Compare their comments:

A John Aldrige says that in the end, Holden remains what he was in the beginning – cynical, defiant, and blind. We feel sorry for Holden, but there is no sense of tragedy because we don't finally care about him enough.

B S. N. Behrman says that Holden knows that things won't remain the same. He has learnt something, though he is not sure what.

C Behrman says: 'One day, Holden will probably find himself in the mood to call up Jane. He may become more tolerant of phonies . . . or even write a novel.'

D Charles Kegel says that Holden will not submit to the phoniness of life, but will attain an attitude of tolerance, understanding, and love. There is no doubt that when he returns home to New York, for he will return home, he will be in the mood to give 'old Jane a buzz'.

1 Which is the most optimistic (positive) view and which is the most pessimistic (negative)?
2 What do you think about the ending?
3 Which of the critics' view do you most agree with?

Activity 2 The last page

Some readers find the ending of the novel very gloomy and pessimistic (negative). Others think it shows Holden in a positive way. Re-read the last page of the novel. What clues are there that the final tone is either optimistic or pessimistic?

Some are already given for you. Decide which column they should be placed in.

Clues that it is an optimistic (positive) ending	Clues that it is a pessimistic (negative) ending

Starting-point statements:

- Holden is in a psychiatric hospital of some kind
- He sounds the same as ever
- He seems to have lost interest in his future

Activity 3 Holden's reply

Imagine you are Holden. Write a one-paragraph letter to the critics telling them whether they were right or wrong about your future. Say what you are doing now, ten years after the ending of the novel. You might start like this:

'You guys all got it wrong. You really wanna know what happened to me . . . ?'

CHARACTERS

Activity 1 Describing the characters

Look at the two tables below. One is a list of some of the characters in the novel. The second is a description of them. Match up the character in table A to the description in table B.

**Table A:
Character list**
Carl Luce
D. B. Caulfield
Holden Caulfield
Maurice
Mr Antolini
Mr Spencer
Phoebe Caulfield
Robert Ackley
Sally Hayes
Sunny
Ward Stradlater

Table B: Character descriptions

Description
A prostitute whom Holden hires for the evening but then rejects; she demands a ten-dollar payment when Holden believes that he is only required to pay five.
An opinionated, obnoxious student at Pencey, he lives in a dorm room connected to the one where Holden lives. He is physically disgusting; his complexion is horrible and Holden suspects that he never brushes his teeth.
Holden goes out on a date with this girl, whose pretentious mannerisms and affectations he dislikes. Despite his contempt for her, Holden asks her to run away with him to New England, where they can live in a cabin in the wilderness together.
Holden's former English teacher at Elkton Hills who now teaches at NYU. He allows Holden to stay with him and his wife after Holden leaves his home. Holden awakes to find him touching his head, which Holden interprets as a homosexual advance, and quickly leaves.
Holden's history teacher at Pencey, he discusses Holden's expulsion with him before he leaves the school, and advises him to get some direction in his life.
Holden's ten-year-old sister, she is more mature and intelligent than her age suggests.
Holden's older brother, he is a war veteran who is currently a scriptwriter in Hollywood.

One of the most intelligent people that Holden knows, he was a student at Whooton when Holden attended, and then went to Columbia. He meets Holden at the Wicker Bar, where he criticizes him for his immature behaviour and recommends that he gets psychiatric help.

The elevator man at the Edmont Hotel who is also a pimp, he assaults Holden after he refuses to pay a ten-dollar fee to the prostitute he arranges for him.

The narrator of *The Catcher in the Rye*, he is the son of a wealthy New York family.

Vain, self-centred, and arrogant but nevertheless a 'secret slob', he is Holden's roommate. He asks Holden to write an English essay for him, but then rejects the essay when it is not to his satisfaction.

Activity 2 Considering the characters

Now look at the character list again. Working in pairs or a small group put them in order of:

Characters we like most ——————— Characters we like least

Activity 3 Holden Caulfield fact-file

How much do we learn about Holden? Use a fact-file like this one to make notes on what we know about him by the end of the novel:

Name:

Age:

Parents:

Brothers/sisters:

Educational background:

Key features of his character:

Likes:

Dislikes:

Activity 4 Reacting to Holden

Readers react differently to Holden's character. Read these two comments from Year 11 students.

Andy: *'I really sympathize with Holden. He's quite insecure but trying hard to work out who he is.'*

Rhianna: *'I lost patience with Holden. He's just too self-centred to be a likeable character.'*

Which opinion do you most agree with, and why?

Activity 5 Casting characters

Imagine that someone is about to make a film of *The Catcher in the Rye*. Think of the main characters:

- Holden Caulfield
- Phoebe Caulfield
- Mr Antolini
- Ward Stradlater

Imagine you are writing notes for a casting director (the person who chooses the actors to play the parts). Your task is to suggest the kinds of looks the actor will need. You might comment on:

- height
- build
- facial features
- hair
- particular mannerisms/behaviour traits

You might want to do a quick sketch, annotated with arrows and labels, to help the casting director. You could also suggest actors who would be well-suited, and why.

THEMES AND SYMBOLS

Activity 1 Loss of innocence

Although he is often foul-mouthed, Holden is very concerned about children. He sees them as innocent and needing protection. Use a spider diagram to list some examples of Holden's attitude to innocence. A few examples are given to get you started:

- Holden tries to erase naughty words from the walls of the elementary school that his sister Phoebe attends.
- Holden dreams of being the catcher in the rye. He has built up a picture around some lines he remembers (inaccurately) from the Robert Burns poem 'Comin' Through the Rye'. Holden imagines a 'catcher' preventing small children from falling off a cliff.

Why do you think Holden feels this way about childhood innocence? What does it tell us about his attitude to adult life?

Write a paragraph about this part of Holden's character.

Activity 2 Rebellion

How much of a rebel is Holden? What is he rebelling against? Think about his attitude to people in the book, to institutions (e.g. schools), to concepts (e.g. adulthood), and about his use of language.

1 Describe four ways in which Holden proves a rebel.
2 What evidence is there that he is less of a rebel than he first appears?

Activity 3 Mental instability

The book begins as Holden is recovering from his nervous breakdown. He tries to save all children from growing up and losing their innocence, and when he realizes that he cannot, he becomes mentally unstable and can't deal with it.

Death is a major issue in this novel because of the death of his brother, Allie. It is the death of his brother which fuels his desire to save children from growing up and becoming corrupt. Holden uses his brother as a model for innocence.

Some of the events of Holden's past appear to have had an influence on his mental state today. Look at the examples below and, for each one, say what you think the effect on him has been.

Event	Effect on Holden	How can you tell?
The death of his brother Allie		
Disliking his parents		
Attending several different private schools		

Activity 4 Relationships

Look at the statements below. Discuss each one in pairs or small groups, and decide whether you think the statement is:

true (T)   possibly true (P)   not true (N)   can't tell (C)

Then write a sentence explaining your choice.

a) No one would choose to be friends with Holden Caulfield.
b) Holden Caulfield is incapable of positive relationships with anyone.
c) Holden hates everyone, including himself.
d) Holden is very immature.

e) Holden is very confident.

f) Holden is likeable underneath the surface.

g) Holden is secretly terrified about sex.

h) Holden sometimes shows commitment to other people.

1   'Phoney' is a key word associated with Holden. A dictionary definition of the word is 'not genuine, a fake; insincere or pretentious'.

Write down a definition which explains what the word means to Holden.

2   Holden uses very colloquial (informal and chatty) language to express his ideas. Read this example:

'He was putting all these dumb, show-offy ripples in the high notes, and a lot of other very tricky stuff that gives me a pain in the ass. You should've heard the crowd, though, when he was finished. You would've puked. They went mad. They were exactly the same morons that laugh like hyenas in the movies at stuff that isn't funny. I swear to God, if I were a piano player or an actor or something and all those dopes thought I was terrific, I'd hate it. I wouldn't even want them to clap for me. People always clap for the wrong things.'

What happens when you put Holden's language into standard English – the kind of language we might expect to be used by newsreaders, teachers, lawyers, and so on? Here's the opening of the extract rewritten. What differences do you notice?

He was putting a lot of foolish, attention-seeking ripples in the high notes, and a lot of other very tricky things that irritate me . . .

a   Rewrite the rest of the paragraph in standard English.

b   Write down the main changes you had to make to:
   ♦   sentences
   ♦   words

c   Re-read your new paragraph. How has the different style changed the character of Holden?

3   *The Catcher in the Rye* was unusual when it was first published because it uses a spoken register. That means it is written as if the character is speaking directly to us.

What are the features that make it feel like spoken language?

Use a checklist like the one below and the paragraph describing Holden's dream. See how many spoken features of language you can come up with.

Features of spoken language	Examples in the extract
Use of informal connectives and fillers – such as *you know, kind of*	
Use of demonstrative adjectives – such as *these* and *those*	
Use of informal vocabulary	
Use of a looser sentence style than you would expect in written language	
More repetition than in written language	

'Anyway, I keep picturing all these little kids playing some game in this big field of rye and all. Thousands of little kids, and nobody's around – nobody big, I mean – except me. And I'm standing on the edge of some crazy cliff. What I have to do, I have to catch everybody if they start to go over the cliff – I mean if they're running and they don't look where they're going I have to come out from somewhere and catch *them. That's all I'd do all day. I'd just be the catcher in the rye and all. I know it's crazy, but that's the only thing I'd really like to be. I know it's crazy.'*

4 How would the novel work if its language was in a written rather than a spoken register? What if it had been written as a diary, for example, or as a series of letters to a friend?

Choose one paragraph from the novel and have a go at rewriting it as if it was a diary entry or letter.

Then write a paragraph describing the changes you had to make to the original, and the difference to the way the text sounds.

5 Since *The Catcher in the Rye* was published, many novels have used a similar style. J. D. Salinger's novel also echoes a much earlier American novel – *The Adventures of Huckleberry Finn* by Mark Twain.

Here are three extracts. One of them is written by J. D. Salinger (in a different novel); one is from *The Adventures of Huckleberry Finn*; one is from Raymond Chandler's *Playback*, a detective novel published in 1958.

See if you can 'spot the Salinger'.

For each text, discuss what features make you think it IS/IS NOT written by Salinger.

You might focus on:

◆ choice of words
◆ the way the narrator addresses the reader
◆ sentence style and length

A

He didn't show. I finished the cigarette, dropped it overboard, and backed out. As I turned out of the driveway towards the town, I saw his car on the other side of the street, parked left hand to the kerb. I kept going, turned right at the boulevard and took it easy so that he wouldn't blow a gasket trying to keep up. There was a restaurant about a mile along called The Epicure. It had a low roof, and a red brick wall to shield it from the street and it had a bar. The entrance was at the side. I parked and went in.

B

I went back into the apartment, very unsteadily, trying to unbutton my tunic as I wandered along, or to yank it open. My return to the living room was unreservedly hailed by my one remaining guest – whom I'd forgotten. He raised a well-filled glass at me as I came into the room. In fact, he literally waved it at me, wagging his head up and down and grinning, as though the supreme, jubilant moment we had both been long awaiting had finally arrived. I found I couldn't quite match grins with him at this particular reunion.

C

Well, three or four months run along, and it was well into the winter, now. I had been to school most all the time, and could spell, and read, and write just a little, and could say the multiplication table up to six times seven is thirty-five, and I don't reckon I could ever get any further than that if I was to live forever. I don't take no stock in mathematics, anyway.

WRITING ABOUT THE NOVEL

Activity 1   Opening paragraphs

A group of students in Year 10 were asked to write a response to this question:

'*The Catcher in the Rye* was written more than half a century ago and yet it still makes a strong impact on many readers. What do you think is its appeal?'

- ◆ How would you structure a response?
- ◆ What would your opening paragraph say?

Read both examples of the students' work and decide which one you think is the more successful opening paragraph.

> ### Student A
> I think The Catcher in the Rye is still a really enjoyable book though it takes quite a while to get into it. I think readers like it because it feels so modern, for example with Holden using lots of words that we still use today. This is definitely one reason for its appeal today.

Student B

The Catcher in the Rye was first published in 1951 and made a huge impact. Readers were both fascinated and shocked by it because it was so different from other novels of the 1950s. There are various reasons that we continue to enjoy the novel today. These include: the character of Holden, the style of the novel, the theme of childhood/adult life.

- ♦ Which do you think more successfully begins to address the question?
- ♦ Which words and phrases would you change?
- ♦ What advice would you give to each student?

Activity 2   Essay endings

What would you expect to see in the final paragraph of an answer to this question? Write down your answer.

Now read these two conclusions, written by different students. The essay question was the same.

Student A

The points in my essay all show different reasons why people still enjoy reading The Catcher in the Rye. Although it is more than 50 years old, it still has a very modern feel. This is in what it says and also in the way it says it.

Student B

There are many reasons that readers continue to enjoy The Catcher in the Rye – from its themes (which still apply today), to the fascinating character of Holden, and its style. For me, it is the style that makes the novel most memorable. It is a written style that continues to feel very fresh and original.

- ♦ Which do you think more successfully concludes the assignment?
- ♦ Which words and phrases would you change?
- ♦ What advice would you give to each student?

SAMPLE ANSWER

Look at this question and think about how you would approach it:

'In what ways does *The Catcher in the Rye* show us the weaknesses of modern society?'

Think about the points you would want to make in your answer.

How would you organize your ideas?

Now look at this complete essay. Read it first covering up the Examiner's comments. See what you think are its strengths and weaknesses in:

- structure
- expression (words and sentences)
- style (e.g. use of quotations)

Then see what the Examiner says.

Sample answer	Comments by Examiner
Holden is a strong critic of society. Many incidents in the novel portray Holden as a person full of hatred towards society There are many traditions that he attacks. He uses the word 'phoney' to describe many of the things he does not like. He thinks everyone he knows or meets are phoneys with the exception of Jane, Allie, and Phoebe. This is because he doesn't like people being insincere and he criticizes society for encouraging people to pretend to be something they are not. In chapter 3, Ackley told Holden, differently every time, that he was supposed to have sex one summer. This is an example of the many people in society, lying and boasting about all kinds of things.	This is a good opening sentence which shows you are addressing the question directly. You are right to use 'phoneys' as a central point, but the first paragraph ought to map out what your answer will cover before discussing this first point.
Holden attacks various weaknesses in our society. He criticizes everything that had happened to him, many of the situations that he has experienced come across in today's society. His point of view on phoneys, losing a loved one, not remembering the true meaning of Christmas, are all the weaknesses in society.	This paragraph doesn't really add anything to your first paragraph.
We begin to understand Holden's reason for hating phoneys. The many people that Holden mentioned were phoneys, one being Ackley. More phoneys were mentioned in this novel than pure and sincere people. Ones classified by Holden as pure and sincere are Jane, Phoebe, Mrs Morrow and the nuns. Holden thinks that there are more phoneys in society than people who are pure. This opinion is true to some and not to others and will remain controversial.	Again, this discusses the same topic ('phoneys') without really adding any new information.
Mr Antolini confronted Holden's belief in death when he said that, 'The mark of the immature man is that he wants to die nobly for a cause, while the mark of the mature man is he wants to live humbly for one'. It is never really clear what Mr Antolini means with his approach to Holden. He was probably showing affection for a boy he knows is lonely and confused. The scene reveals that Holden doesn't accept homosexuals. The stroking of Holden's head awakened him, Holden immediately jumped to conclusions before even thinking of reasons. He may be criticizing the way men behave, or the way society won't let men show emotions to one another.	This paragraph starts very abruptly. There is a good point here about what Mr Antolini represents, but it isn't explored in enough detail. You need to show more clearly that you're talking about society and not just a character point.

Sample answer	Comments by Examiner
Christmas is another tradition that Holden attacks. Christmas to Holden is nothing but depression because he knows what others think, people have forgot the real meaning of Christmas. Holden's point of view is agreeable, people worry more about what to give to others and what to receive from others, that they tend to forget the real meaning of Christmas.	This is a fair point but lacks a specific example.
Even though Holden criticizes so much in life, he is still mostly right about society. As a 16-year-old boy, he seems to understand the society better than most people. He attacks a level of phoniness that is even more around today.	This conclusion tries to pull the main strands of the essay together. The final sentence needs a bit more explanation.

Conclusion

There are many good points in this answer, and it demonstrates an understanding of the novel. It is not very well organized, however, and leaves out many relevant points. Perhaps most importantly, it lacks quotations. This makes it seem too generalized because you don't give specific examples to support your points.

Work likely to be produced by a C grade candidate.

6 WRITING TO ARGUE, PERSUADE, AND ADVISE

How to study the features of different text types

How to write persuasive texts

In this unit you will develop these skills:

SPEAKING AND LISTENING	READING	WRITING	LANGUAGE WORKSHOP
Discussing different text types	Reading different examples of persuasive writing	Writing to argue, persuade, advise	Exploring personal and impersonal writing
For coursework assessment of your contribution to a group discussion	For English paper 1, section A	For English paper 1, section B	To get the style right for the writing task in section B

INTRODUCTION

We are surrounded by texts which aim to persuade or advise us, or which aim to argue a case. They include:

- letters
- speeches
- posters
- pamphlets and leaflets
- newspaper and magazine articles

Paper 1 of your English exam will require you to be able to write a good persuasive text. This unit shows you some good examples of persuasive writing and helps you to develop the necessary skills.

Activity 1 Exploring different text types

1 Here are some examples of the kinds of task you might be expected to write in the examination. They are all taken from AQA past papers.

Spend a few minutes looking down the list.

- Which do you think you would find easiest to write? Why?
- Which do you think you would find most difficult? Why?

Writing to argue

a) Write an article for a teenage magazine in which you **argue** the case for more help to be given to the homeless.

b) Write an article for a magazine aimed at parents. **Argue** the case either for or against children being allowed to have a television in their bedrooms to watch whatever they like, whenever they like.

c) Write a letter to your MP in which you **argue** either for or against animal experimentation.

d) Write an article suitable for a school magazine in which you **argue** that more should be done in school to improve the health and fitness of pupils.

e) How useful do you think it is to know about the past? Write an article for a newspaper in which you **argue** your case.

Writing to persuade

f) A friend has written you a letter saying he or she is thinking of leaving home and is asking for your advice. Write a reply trying to **persuade** him or her not to leave home.

g) Your Headteacher has decided not to spend any more money on buying televisions for use in school classrooms. Write a letter **persuading** him or her that television plays a very important part in education.

h) Write an article for a newsletter in which you aim to **persuade** your readers that animals should be released from any form of captivity.

i) Write a letter to your local paper in which you try to **persuade** the readers more bike-friendly measures should be introduced in your area.

j) Write an article for a television magazine to **persuade** readers to watch a programme called *The death of the dinosaurs: a mystery solved*.

k) Write the text for a travel brochure published by a run-down seaside resort which aims to **persuade** holiday-makers to return by using an original and imaginative selling point.

Writing to advise

l) Your class has been invited to the local TV studio to form part of the audience in a discussion programme. Write a set of guidelines in which you **advise** the students on exactly what they will need to do on the day of their visit.

m) Write a leaflet for pedestrians and road users in which you **advise** them about road safety.

n) Write a leaflet for new pet owners in which you **advise** them on the requirements of looking after an animal of your choice.

o) Write a leaflet in which you **advise** students how to use the facilities of a library, or resource centre, for a research project.

p) Write a leaflet for the public, **advising** them how to have a safe day out at the beach.

2 What do you understand by the key terms, *argue, persuade, advise*? How do their meanings differ? Look at the list of tasks above and the definitions below, and use a chart like this to help you pin down their meanings:

	Argue	Persuade	Advise
Definition:			
Used in these text types:			

a) Definition – which goes with which heading?

- ◆ Aims to help someone decide what to do
- ◆ Aims to get someone to do something
- ◆ Aims to put forward a point of view

b) What types of texts do you expect under each heading? (Some of these may appear under several headings)

- ◆ leaflet
- ◆ newspaper report
- ◆ speech
- ◆ advice sheet
- ◆ letter
- ◆ brochure

3 What will be the biggest challenge for you? Look at this self-assessment grid to assess your own strengths and weaknesses:

	Strength	Needs some work	Weakness
Getting the style right			
Working in exam conditions			
Organizing the writing			
Using the right kind of vocabulary			
Making my writing interesting enough			

The rest of this unit gives you advice on all of these areas.

Activity 2 Looking at leaflets / advice sheets / brochures

These texts use words and design features to persuade, argue or advise. Design features might include:

- ◆ use of colour
- ◆ font styles and sizes
- ◆ images
- ◆ shading, boxes, lines
- ◆ text organization (e.g. bullet points and short paragraphs).

Alex Cubitt writes leaflets. Here's her advice on creating a good leaflet:

Keep it simple. Don't overdo the use of colour or images. Some of the worst leaflets have too much happening – too many font styles, and they become confusing and cheap-looking. In my leaflets I try to keep lots of white space so that the text really stands out, and I use images to help explain my points – not just to make it all look pretty! The writing is really important. Don't spend all your time on the visuals. Make sure you choose clear language, short sentences, bullet points, and short paragraphs.

Look at this leaflet produced for Pentax:

Essential Skills

Now you're the proud owner of a brand new camera, you'll naturally want to load a roll of film into it and start taking lots of great pictures.

The good news is that's exactly what you can do. The beauty of 'point-and-shoot' compact cameras like this is they're easy to use. Once the batteries and film are loaded, everything is taken care of so all you have to do is compose an interesting picture then press the shutter release button. Focusing and exposure are both automatic, and if light levels are low the built-in flash will cut-in to light your subject.

Saying that, if you want to get the best possible results from your camera, there are a few factors you should consider.

Camera handling

People hold cameras in lots of strange ways, but the most effective and comfortable is to grip the body either side, as shown, so your right finger falls naturally over the shutter release button. Take care not to obscure the flash with your left hand as this will affect the results.

The camera should also be held close to your eye so you can see clearly through the viewfinder, with the body resting against your cheek for support.

Which format?

Most pictures are taken with the camera held horizontally in the 'landscape' format. This is mainly due to the fact that cameras are easier to hold this way, but also

because for scenic pictures, the horizontal format is more suitable.

However, in many instances, the upright format will be more appropriate, so remember to turn your camera on its side from time to time.

This approach is better for portraiture as the human body forms an upright shape – if you use the camera horizontally for portraits you'll end up with lots of wasted space either side of your subject – and a weak picture.

It can also be used for pictures of tall buildings, or anything else that would fill an upright picture.

Take care with focusing

If you have an autofocus camera, you'll need to make sure that the camera focuses on the important part of the scene. Most of the time this is no problem, as it's at the centre of the picture, which is where the sensor reads from.

But you can have difficulties when photographing two people side-by-side, as the sensor can go between their heads, and expose the background rather than them.

In such situations, either ask your subjects to move in close together, or use the camera's focus-lock. To do this, place the central area of the viewfinder over one of the faces, press down the shutter half-way and hold, and then re-frame the shot.

Selective Enlarging

The great advantage of having a wide-angle lens on your camera is that it allows you to photograph groups of people, large buildings and vast panoramas with ease.

Sometimes, though, you want to concentrate on just part of the

scene, and in situations like this you can always ask your processing lab to make a 'selective' enlargement, blowing up just part of the picture to give it more impact. That's what we've done with some of the pictures in this booklet, to enable you to enjoy them better, and it will work just as well with your pictures too.

1 Working in pairs, use a table like the one below to assess how successful it is. Use another table to evaluate a different leaflet – e.g. for homework.

Key features	Pentax leaflet	
Purpose: to argue, persuade, or advise (and how can you tell)?		
Design features – e.g. ◆ colour ◆ use of images ◆ organization of text	Strengths	Weaknesses
Use of language – e.g. ◆ use of subheadings ◆ clarity of writing ◆ interest level	Strengths	Weaknesses
How effective is the leaflet?	1 (not very) ————— 5 (very)	
How could it be improved?		

2 Now look at this example of an unsuccessful leaflet. Its task is to persuade students to cut their fat intake. Using the arrows to guide you, make a list of points to show what is wrong with it.

Images

Headline

CUT DOWN YOUR FAT
Eating fat isn't good for you so you should try to cut down the amount of fat you eat. Fat includes things like red meat and chocolate and also most dairy products. You should aim to eat less of these so that your body is healthier.

Text

Chips
If you eat lots of chips and things like that every day then you may be eating too much fat. Chips are not healthy because they are fried in fat. In fact sometimes they are double fried to make them crispy. Although this can taste nice it means that chips contain loads of fat and this can damage your heart.

Sub-head

Pumps
Your heart pumps the blood around your body. If you eat too much fat it starts to get clogged up and this means it has to work harder to pump the blood. The more fat you eat, the more you will clog up your heart. This can lead to heart disease, so you should be careful what you eat.

Snack attack
Also remember that chocolate and crisps may taste good for a breaktime snack but they also contain a lot of fat. You should try to eat less chocolate and crisps and instead eat fresh fruit.

Persuasiveness

Take this advice or you could die.

3 Decide what is wrong with this leaflet. Is there anything you like about it?

4 Design your own leaflet to persuade students to eat more healthily.

Before you start, plan your leaflet. Refer back to Alex Cubitt's advice on page 81.

Activity 3 Looking at speeches

Speeches are still an important part of government. Local and national politicians use speeches to inform people about their ideas, and to persuade us that they are the right ideas. People hear speeches on the news, at meetings, in assemblies, and in church. We also read them in newspaper articles and on websites.

What makes a good speech?

Read this example by Prime Minister Tony Blair and see how successful you think it is. The speech was made in the House of Commons. Its aim was to persuade MPs that the Government's approach to health was proving successful.

Explore the language of the speech using the numbered questions on the next page.

STATEMENT ON HEALTH POLICY MADE BY THE PRIME MINISTER
Delivered in the Commons 22 March 2000

1   Everybody knows that the NHS needed the new money announced yesterday.

But everybody knows too that the NHS needs fundamental reform if it is to provide the standard of care people deserve in the 21st century.

2   With the money, must come the modernization.

3   A step change in resources must mean a step change in reform.

In our schools, we now accept that though more investment is necessary, it is not sufficient. There is a real and often hard debate about standards, performance, and reform.

No-one really believes that one without the other will work.

Now is the time to raise the same debate in our NHS.

4   So this afternoon, I will set out the key challenges facing the Health Service, the means by which we intend to tackle them and the methods for involving the people who work in the Health Service in this vital task.

5   I say to our hard-working and dedicated staff in the NHS: You challenged us to come up with the money. We have done so. It was hard won and hard fought. There were many calls on it. Many places it might have been spent. We rose to your challenge. Now rise to ours. Work with us to make sure this money is spent well; make sure the NHS confronts the hard necessities of reform to improve the value we get for the money we spend.

1 Why do you think he says 'everybody' instead of 'I' or 'we'?
2 Why do you think he uses the two words 'money' and 'modernization'?
3 Why do think he repeats the phrase 'step change'?
4 Why do you think he tells his audience what he is going to tell them?
5 Why do you think he addresses these people directly?

Talking points

1 Which of these techniques do you think is the most noticeable feature in Tony Blair's speech? Which is the least noticeable?
a) Repetition of key words and phrases
b) Short sentences
c) Emotional words (e.g. challenge)
d) Addressing different parts of the audience directly
e) Simple language

2 How can you tell that he is trying to PERSUADE his audience about something, rather than simply inform them?
3 What do you think works well in the speech? What is unsuccessful?

Writing a speech

Now look at this example. It was written in response to this exam question on Paper 1:

'Write a speech for your MP to use when he or she is going to persuade fellow MPs to vote for more money being made available for foreign aid.'

What do you think is wrong with the speech?

Dear fellow MPs

As you all know we are a very rich country. In fact we are very rich indeed. We have microwaves and DVD players. Some people in the world are not very rich at all and we need to help them, yes help them. We have a duty to help them and we should give them some foreign aid. Foreign aid is money that we use to help people abroad.

I strongly urge you to vote for giving more money to people who are in need. We are all part of the same world and it is not right that some people should go without nice things because we are too greedy to help them.

So I beg you to support me tonight and vote for more money as foreign aid.

Thank you

1 This speech was written by a Year 10 student called Becky. How would you advise her to improve her speech? Use the sentence prompts below to advise her:

- The main problem with your speech is . . .
- To make the speech more persuasive you should . . .
- You do use some repetition of words. Now you should try . . .
- Look at some of the vocabulary you use. You should try to . . .
- Look at your use of personal pronouns (*I, me, we*). You should try to . . .

2 Now, to demonstrate to Becky how she could create a more successful speech, take the same topic and write the opening **three** paragraphs of a speech.

3 Then, underneath your sample speech, use **three to five** bullet points to list the key features you have used to make it successful.

Activity 4 Writing persuasive letters

Letters can be a useful way of trying to persuade a reader to support you, or to buy something. A lot of direct mailing ('junk mail') uses personalized letters as an approach. Direct mailing means the letters contain the name of the person who owns the house, and they can seem more personal than a general letter. Look at the difference a personal address can make:

> Dear Mr Barton
>
> As a previous customer at Jam Online, you'll be delighted to hear that our Autumn sale has just begun . . .

> Dear Householder
>
> Have you thought about the money that's currently escaping through your roof? If you haven't insulated your loft, then you could be losing up to £50 a week!

Letters allow charities, companies, even political parties to address the reader directly. Sometimes letters will be official and formal; at other times they may be deeply personal.

This letter was written by two inmates of Death Row in Alabama, USA: Wallace Thomas and Jesse Morrison. They wrote an open letter to society to persuade people that the death penalty is unfair.

As you read it, look at how the writers use language to persuade their readers that the death penalty is wrong. Use the question prompts to guide you.

1 We, the inmates of Alabama's Death Row, have been portrayed as animals unfit for society. We have loved ones and families who have suffered as much as anyone. We have sat here for years, praying and hoping for positive results. The only time we are heard is during our trials and hours before we are electrocuted. However, we are human beings also. We have mothers, fathers, sisters, brothers, daughters, sons, nieces and nephews who are affected as much as those of us who sit here on Death Row. The death penalty has destroyed family members, caused many to lose jobs, and caused others to relocate and begin life again. It has caused our children to be singled out and humiliated in school. The death penalty has caused legal, economic, social and psychological problems for us and our families which can never be resolved.

2 Many of us have made mistakes as humans will err; many of us regret these mistakes, and many of us have learned from these mistakes. All of us want and need the opportunity to prove to society that we can be productive citizens who can contribute to this society in a positive fashion.

3 We wonder how much hate and vengefulness the American nation will endure before its citizens stand up and say that enough is enough. We are the only civilized and free country in the world which says that if a person makes a mistake at the tender age of 16, he must die for it. We are the only civilized and free country in the world which says that we will stop murder by murdering in the name of justice, and we are the only free country which says that if a person is not the right color and has no money, the chances are that he will never encounter justice.

4 The death penalty cannot cure ills that won't go away. We must seek lasting solutions that will make us a better people. We must start by abolishing the death penalty.

5 We ask you in the name of love, peace and true justice to lift every voice and demand an end to the death penalty in the United States of America.

1 How do the writers aim to build our sympathy for them?
2 How do they create a positive image of the inmates?
3 The writers change topic in this paragraph. What is their topic?
4 How do the writers try to persuade readers that things must change?
5 How do the writers make their style much more direct?

Talking points

Which of these techniques is most important and least important in making the letter persuade us?

- a mixture of short and longer sentences
- repetition of emotive words
- use of connectives to organize the arguments (e.g. *however*)
- use of first person plural (*we*) and second person (*you*) to involve the reader
- use of facts and statistics
- use of personal information
- use of modal verb *must* to add power to the argument

Complete these sentences:

The most important technique is . . .
The least important technique is . . .

Letters are not always as personal as this. Sometimes they give more general advice and information.

Here is advice from the Plain English Society on the ingredients of a good letter:

Plain English Campaign

As everyone always says, a letter needs a beginning, middle and end. Much of the time, your letter should start 'Thank you for your letter of 15 April' and certainly not 'I acknowledge receipt of . . .', 'I am in receipt of . . .' or 'Further to your recent . . . .'

The middle will be your points, answers and questions in a logical order. If it is a long letter, you may be able to break it up using sub-headings. Use paragraphing throughout, generally averaging about three or four sentences to each paragraph.

The end does not normally need to be a summary. A suitable final sentence might be 'I hope this has answered your questions', 'Thank you for your help' or 'If you have any questions, please ring me.'

The rest of this section is taken up entirely with suggestions. Some of them may be very obvious to you while others may go against your own style. They are only suggestions.

The date
It is now common practice to write the date as 7 July 1991 instead of 7th July 1991.

The greeting
If you are on first name terms with the reader, use 'Dear Jane'. Otherwise use 'Dear Mr Smith', 'Dear Miss Smith' or if you are writing to a woman and don't know which title she prefers, use 'Dear Ms Smith'. If you don't know the person's name, use 'Dear Sir', 'Dear Madam' or occasionally 'Dear Sir or Madam'.

Headings
These are not usually necessary. However, if you are going to use one, don't use all capitals; just put the heading in bold. And don't use 're'.

Punctuation
Don't put commas after:

◆ each line of the address;
◆ the greeting (Dear Jane); or
◆ the ending line (Yours sincerely).

Also, you don't need full stops in initials – Mr P D Smith, the DSS and so on.

Endings
If you start 'Dear name' end 'Yours sincerely'. Otherwise, end with 'Yours faithfully'.

Contact point
Make sure that your letter clearly says which person the reader should contact and how, with any extension number if necessary.

Emphasising words
If you want to emphasise something, use bold type. Don't use long strings of capital letters as they are unfriendly and many people find them much harder to read.

Always read your letter when you have finished.

Check that:

◆ you have said everything you wanted to;
◆ you have answered any questions you had to;
◆ you have been helpful and polite; and
◆ the letter is clear and concise.

Studying an example of a persuasive letter

Here is an extract from an unsuccessful letter. It was written in response to this question:

'Write a letter to your MP saying that you think people should not be allowed to keep exotic pets like snakes and crocodiles.'

Dear MP

I think it is totally wrong that people are allowed to keep exotic pets. It is cruel and unfair. How would you like it if you were a snake used to crawling around a jungle one day and the next day stuck in a glass cage in someone's bedroom.

Something should be done about this and that is why I am writing to you.

Yours sincerely,

Jake Lees.

1   Make a list of **five** things that you think are wrong with this letter.

2   Using the letter-writing hints above, write a better letter to your MP on the same topic.

Activity 5 Writing articles

Articles in newspapers and magazines can be written for a range of purposes.

News articles are chiefly written:

- to entertain (e.g. a gossipy article about a celebrity)
- to inform (e.g. an article giving information about health issues)

Features articles are sometimes written:

- to persuade (e.g. a leader article telling readers how they should vote at the next election)
- to advise (e.g. an article on which MP3 player is best value)
- to argue (e.g. an opinion article commenting on a new film)

Persuasive articles will often use a different structure from news articles. They do not aim to be balanced and objective. Instead they want to shape our opinions.

Look at these extracts from different styles of persuasive articles. They are on a range of serious and light-hearted topics.

1   For each one, decide how you can tell that it is designed to persuade, argue, or advise.

A

Pop Idol, the latest offering in the relentless copycat production line of embarrassment TV, leaves me totally cold. Did around 10 million people really tune in? And did 5.8 million people really feel the need to call in on Saturday to support either Will, Gareth or Darius (yes the very same Darius from Popstars – he doesn't give up easily, that one)?

OK, so a fair percentage of those votes can be easily explained. Each contestant has his fair share of relatives, friends and student buddies who are prepared to vote 20 or 30 times, minimum. But it still doesn't explain the millions of other votes.

B

Helping the Rich, Harming the Poor

5th November, 2001

By Sebastian Mallaby

Here's some of why we have an image problem in the world's poor nations. Some 2.8 billion people subsist on less than $2 a day. We in the rich world preach that if they work hard they will climb out of poverty. But then we impose our highest import taxes on precisely those industries in which most of the poor work – farming and low-tech manufacturing.

Because of this discrimination, the average worker in the poor world faces tariffs roughly twice as high as the average worker in rich countries, according to the World Bank.

C

Until about ten years ago, skiing was the normal thing to do, and there are still more skiers than snowboarders.

Skiing is more difficult to learn because you have to control two planks on your feet rather than just one. But it has become a lot easier in recent years thanks to rapidly improving technology – basically skis have got shorter and wider, and are much easier to control and have fun on than they used to be. And while a few years ago snowboarding was much trendier among the younger age group, skiing has now become cool again – many snowboarders are moving on to skis because of their extra manoeuvrability and the flexibility they give you to move easily all over the mountain.

It is, however, much easier and quicker to grasp the basics of snowboarding than skiing. With skiing you are likely to need at least a few weeks on skis to get to a stage where you feel confident about trying all the runs on the mountain, especially the steeper ones or off-piste.

2 Which extract most makes you want to keep reading? Why – is it because of the topic, or the style?

A good persuasive article should include:

- facts and statistics
- an attention-grabbing opening
- a lively style
- a mix of short and long sentences
- an argument that is clearly organized
- understandable vocabulary

3 Read this article about young people and exercise. It was written in response to this task:

'Many people think young people should do more exercise. Write an article for a school newspaper in which you try to persuade students to get more exercise.'

Decide what you think could be improved in the article.

Exercise for Health
By Helen Morley

I think you need to think carefully about what you eat and how you exercise. It is really easy to get into bad habits by travelling to school every day by car or bus and not really get enough exercise. If you do this you will stop being fit and you will find that you are less successful at school.

A healthy body leads to a healthy mind and if you can find time to do more exercise each day then you will probably find that you are better able to concentrate in lessons. You will also feel better about yourself so it is a good idea to get more exercise.

For more information about exercise go to the PE Department.

What should Helen do to improve this article?

Finish these sentence starters:

- Your headline would be better if . . .
- The article would be better if . . .
- To improve the structure of the article, you should . . .
- To improve your sentences, you should . . .
- To improve your vocabulary, you should . . .

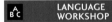

Personal or impersonal language?

One of the decisions to make when writing persuasive texts is how personal or impersonal to make your tone.

Here are the differences:

- First-person mode is the most personal style. It uses the pronouns *I* and *me*.
- Second-person mode addresses the audience directly. It uses the pronoun *you*.
- Third-person mode avoids personal involvement. It uses pronouns such as *it, they,* and *them* and creates a more detached, impersonal tone.

Read these examples:

First person	Second person	Third person
I think it is terrible that animals are transported for hundreds of miles in this way.	You may not know the truth about animal transportation. When did you last think about the issue?	Tens of thousands of animals – chiefly sheep, pigs, and chickens – are transported across Europe every day. They are subjected to terrible conditions.
Good for: adding a personal note to articles	Good for: getting the audience involved	Good for: making your writing formal, authoritative, and impersonal

Active or passive?

A second technique for making your writing personal or impersonal is to think about whether to use the active or passive voice.

Passive verbs are useful when you want to emphasize what is done rather than who is doing it, or if you want your writing to sound factual and detached. But they can sound a little boring and impersonal.

Active verbs express ideas more directly.

Take these examples:

Active

- We should not tolerate animal cruelty. (Active – notice the *we* which makes it more personal)
- We will consider this matter soon.

Passive

- Animal cruelty should not be tolerated. (Passive – it avoids the *we*)
- This matter will be considered soon.

Decide how personal or impersonal you want your text to be.

Activity 6 Building your reading skills

This article from a news website gives more information about the need for school pupils to exercise. Read the text and then answer the questions.

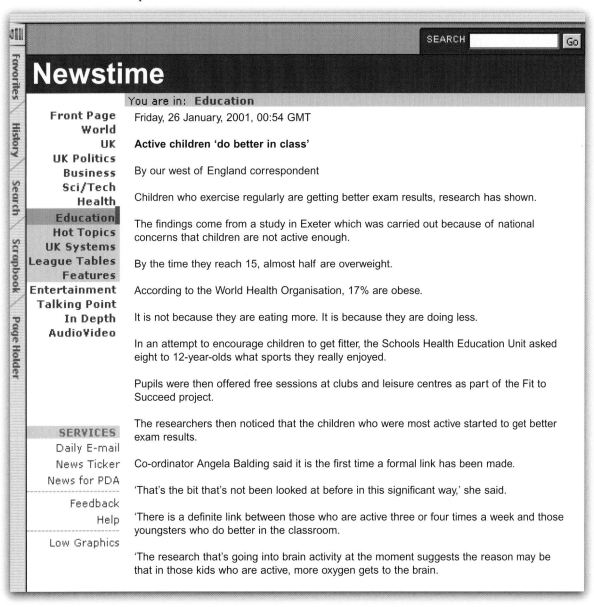

Newstime

SEARCH [   ] Go

Favorites | History | Search | Scrapbook | Page Holder

You are in: **Education**

Front Page
World
UK
UK Politics
Business
Sci/Tech
Health
Education
Hot Topics
UK Systems
League Tables
Features
Entertainment
Talking Point
In Depth
AudioVideo

Friday, 26 January, 2001, 00:54 GMT

Active children 'do better in class'

By our west of England correspondent

Children who exercise regularly are getting better exam results, research has shown.

The findings come from a study in Exeter which was carried out because of national concerns that children are not active enough.

By the time they reach 15, almost half are overweight.

According to the World Health Organisation, 17% are obese.

It is not because they are eating more. It is because they are doing less.

In an attempt to encourage children to get fitter, the Schools Health Education Unit asked eight to 12-year-olds what sports they really enjoyed.

Pupils were then offered free sessions at clubs and leisure centres as part of the Fit to Succeed project.

The researchers then noticed that the children who were most active started to get better exam results.

Co-ordinator Angela Balding said it is the first time a formal link has been made.

'That's the bit that's not been looked at before in this significant way,' she said.

'There is a definite link between those who are active three or four times a week and those youngsters who do better in the classroom.

'The research that's going into brain activity at the moment suggests the reason may be that in those kids who are active, more oxygen gets to the brain.

SERVICES
Daily E-mail
News Ticker
News for PDA

Feedback
Help

Low Graphics

SEARCH [_____] Go

Newstime

You are in: **Education**

'The brain is then better equipped to take more in and be receptive to new things.'
The most dramatic benefits were found among boys.

Of 11-year-olds who scored above average in national English tests, 79% were exercising three times a week.

Of those who scored below average, only 38% were exercising.

One of the schools taking part in the study was St Michael's Church of England Middle School in Exeter.

The headmaster Tim Walker said the results could lead to changes in the national curriculum.

'It may be that PE has to become a core subject and have the status and time allocation that the so-called academic subjects like English, maths and IT already have,' he said.

'Its value to children's academic progress has been proved by the Fit to Succeed programme – now the study is being extended there will be the chance to provide even more data which will back what's already been found out.'

But keeping children interested in sport as they grow older is a big problem.

Girls in particular tend to stop exercising once they reach secondary school.

But the researchers found they were more likely to take part if they were allowed to play traditional 'boys' ' games, such as touch rugby, football and baseball.

'One of the key things that came out of the research that surprised me as a sports development officer was that there was a very strong interest in martial arts among girls and boys,' said Exeter City Council's Kevin Hack.

'The curse of the 21st Century is that many children prefer sitting at their computers, on the internet or watching television.

'The challenge for us is to provide activities that appeal to them enough to get them away from their screens and get them to do something active.'

At the moment PE is compulsory, but it is up to each school to allocate the time.

It could be taken more seriously by showing it has educational as well as health benefits.

FOUNDATION

1 Write down **three** facts about children's health according to the article.
2 Explain, using your own words, what benefits in school more exercise might have.
3 What challenges do schools face in encouraging students to take more exercise?

1   Write down **three** facts about children's health according to the article.

2   Explain the challenges that schools face in encouraging students to take more exercise. Are these different for girls compared to boys?

3   Do you think the writer of this article is neutral, or can her opinions be detected? Explain your answer with examples.

E X A M   H I N T S

Organize your answers clearly. Never waste time writing out the question.

Aim instead to use key words from the question at the start of your answer – e.g. 'Schools face a number of challenges . . .'

Set out your answers with spaces between each one so that the examiner can easily see how you've organized things.

Longer answers need to be organized into paragraphs. It can be easy to forget this under exam pressure.

Activity 7   Building your writing skills

Take the website article and use it to create either a persuasive article, speech, or leaflet.

◆ Your article should encourage students at your school to find ways of taking more exercise.

◆ Your speech should be for an MP to use in Parliament. The aim should be to make PE a core subject of the National Curriculum.

◆ Your leaflet should aim to help students recognize ways of getting more exercise.

➡ For each text type, turn back to the advice panels earlier in this unit.

➡ Refer to the website article on pages 93–4 so that you can quote facts and figures.

E X A M   H I N T S

Spend time planning before you begin to write. Structure is just as important as the words you choose.

Don't worry too much about the layout of your work. Some students find it easier to make their work look like a leaflet or newspaper article on the page, but it's the writing that will get you marks, not the design. Don't waste time on layout features.

Remember that persuasive writing often expresses strong opinions in a controlled way. You need to get the tone right here. If it is too personal ('I think it's terrible that . . .') then you probably need to rethink the tone you are adopting.

SAMPLE ANSWER

Writing a persuasive article

Look at this answer to the exam question 'Write a persuasive article for a teenage fashion magazine about whether following fashion is important'. Read the answer on the left-hand side of the page, keeping the Examiner's comments covered. Decide what you think about the answer first.

Sample answer	Comments by Examiner
Whether or not you choose to follow fashion depends very much on your own perceptions. Some people are content to wear whatever is cheapest. Others look for practicality when buying clothes, preferring something sturdy to something that is currently being paraded on catwalks around the globe. For other people however, it is necessary to be seen in the very latest clothing – whatever the cost.	This opening is all right, but it could be more punchy. 'Perceptions' is a high-level word, but is it appropriate in this context? Good balance of different opinions before you lead into your own views.
Companies are fully aware of the corporate benefits of peer pressure. They know that if one or two members of a group are seen wearing their brand, then the others will almost inevitably buy the same product to 'fit in' with their friends. This is particularly true in a school environment, where peer pressure is inevitably more intense.	
My argument would be this: if you can afford to spend lots of money on fashionable clothes then good for you, but you should be aware that not everyone can, and should never make somebody feel alienated or treat somebody differently because they are wearing different clothes to you. I would also urge people to look carefully at the reasons they are buying clothes. If you want to treat yourself to a new outfit, then go ahead, but choose the things that suit you, that you can afford, and you like.	Perhaps too much use of the personal pronouns *I* and *me* here. It would have more power with less personal opinion.
Do not be fooled by brand names. If you believe that buying the latest Calvin Klein jeans will bring you happiness, and improve your relationships with your friends, then you are mistaken. Any good friend will look past what you are wearing, and judge you by your personality. If you have problems with your relationships with people, then spending lots of money on designer clothing is not going to help you at all. You would be better off spending your money on something that you can enjoy with your mates.	Good use of an imperative sentence – 'Do not be fooled'. There's a lively sense of your personal opinion here, and it is powerfully expressed.
In conclusion, I do not believe that it is a waste of money to follow fashion. This is provided you are doing it for yourself, because you like the clothing. Following fashion becomes a criminal waste of money however, when the clothes are not bought because you like them, but because your mates do or because you want to fit in.	The conclusion is weaker. An article in a magazine wouldn't say 'In conclusion'. It sounds too much like a formal essay.

Conclusion

This is a well-argued piece of persuasive writing, though it sometimes reads more like an essay than an article. It puts together several relevant arguments and presents them in a way that is likely to capture the reader's attention. The mix of statements ('Companies are fully aware . . .') and commands ('Do not be fooled . . .') adds variety to the writing. It is also clearly structured as well as precisely expressed.

Work likely to be produced by an A grade candidate.

7 WRITING TO INFORM, EXPLAIN, AND DESCRIBE

How to analyse the structure and language of informative texts

How to write high-quality descriptive texts

In this unit you will develop these skills:

SPEAKING AND LISTENING	READING	WRITING	LANGUAGE WORKSHOP
Discussing different text types	Reading informative texts – e.g. newspapers and leaflets	Writing to inform, explain, describe	Exploring structure
For coursework assessment of your contribution to a group discussion	For English paper 1, section A	For English paper 2, section B	To get the style right for the writing task in section B

INTRODUCTION

This unit explores writing which is designed to inform, explain, and describe. This might include the following text types:

- ◆ letters
- ◆ travel writing
- ◆ articles
- ◆ autobiography
- ◆ essays
- ◆ leaflets

Paper 2 of your English exam will require you to be able to write a good informative or descriptive text. This unit shows you some good examples of these kinds of writing and helps you to develop the necessary skills.

Activity 1   Exploring different text types

1   Here are some examples of the kinds of task you might be expected to write in the examination. They are all taken from AQA past papers.

Spend a few minutes looking down the list.

- ◆ Which do you think you would find easiest to write? Why?
- ◆ Which do you think you would find most difficult? Why?

Writing to inform

a)   Write a letter to a friend who has recently moved away from your area, **informing** him or her of recent events in your life and the plans for the next few months. Your letter should be lively and interesting.

b) People often enjoy reading about the interests and hobbies of others. Choose something you are interested in and know a lot about. Write about this in a way which will **inform** other people.

c) People of the future may well wonder what life was like at the start of the new millennium. Write an **informative** article for teenagers to read in a hundred years' time. The subject of your article is 'The Life of a Teenager in the year 2000'.

d) Write an **informative** article for teachers about 'Clothes and Today's Teenager.'

e) Your Headteacher has asked Year 11 students to write something for a magazine for new Year 7 students and their parents. Write an article for this magazine in which you **inform** them of the things you think they need to know about your school.

f) Many people are fascinated by animals. Write an article for a wildlife magazine in which you **inform** the readers about the reasons for this fascination and about your own feelings about animals.

Writing to explain

g) Many families have their own particular traditions. These may be to do with how they celebrate holidays, religious festivals, or particular times of the year. Write about your family traditions and **explain** their importance to you.

h) Choose an event from your past that has particular significance for you. **Explain** what happened and your feelings about it.

i) Decisions can be difficult to make. Think about a difficult decision you have had to make. **Explain** what the decision was and what happened as a result of it.

j) There are many pressures on young people today. **Explain** what you think are the main pressures and how they affect your life and the lives of people you know.

k) Friends sometimes play an important part in people's lives. **Explain** what part they play in your life, and explain how important friends are to you.

l) Choose someone or something about which your views have changed as you have got older. Write about what you used to think and feel, what you now think and feel, and **explain** how the change has come about.

Writing to describe

m) **Describe** one of the following in such a way that it can easily be imagined by your reader: a city at night; a deserted beach; a busy shopping centre.

n) Journeys can be exciting, boring, or a mixture of both. **Describe** a journey you have made, so that the reader can imagine it clearly.

o) **Describe** your ideal home.

p) **Describe** your ideal holiday place.

q) Places can seem different at different times of the year. Choose one of the following places: a school playground; a High Street; a pond; a country lane. **Describe** it in winter and summer.

r) To be part of a crowd can be an exciting, frustrating, or frightening experience. **Describe** a crowd scene, focusing on the people, the atmosphere, and the emotions. It could be: at a football ground; at an open-air concert; at a demonstration; somewhere else.

2 What do you understand by the key terms, *inform, explain, describe*? How do their meanings differ? Look at the list of tasks above and the definitions below, and use a chart like this to help you pin down their meanings.

	Inform	**Explain**	**Describe**
Definition:			
Used in these text types:			

a) Definition – which goes with which heading?

- Aims to show what something is like in detail
- Aims to give the reader facts or opinions
- Aims help the reader understand a process

b) What types of texts do you expect under each heading? (Some of these may appear under several headings.)

- letters
- articles
- essays
- travel writing
- autobiography
- leaflets

3 What will be the biggest challenge for you? Look at this self-assessment grid to assess your own strengths and weaknesses.

	Strength	**Needs some work**	**Weakness**
Getting the style right			
Working in exam conditions			
Organizing the writing			
Using the right kind of vocabulary			
Making my writing interesting enough			

The rest of this unit gives you advice on all of these areas.

WRITING TO INFORM

It is always important to consider the purpose and audience of an information text:

- Letters communicate information to people.
- Articles might inform and entertain people.
- Essays might express facts, opinions, and ideas.
- Travel writing informs readers about places.
- Autobiography informs people about the writer's life.
- Leaflets inform and sometimes persuade people about topics and issues.

Focus on newspapers

At weekends, some newspapers aim to inform their readers about people that have been in the news. Instead of telling a story, they give information about that person's life and background.

Early in 2002 the singer Kylie Minogue was in the news for a performance she gave at the annual BRIT Awards.

The *Independent* journalist, David Lister, wrote a profile of Kylie Minogue. Next to it was a list of facts and opinions about Kylie. Look at the two styles of informative writing, which are shown overleaf.

Text A Profiling people

23 February 2002

Kylie Minogue:

Goddess of the moment

BY DAVID LISTER

KYLIE ANN MINOGUE was born 33 years ago in Melbourne, the first child of Carol, a former ballet dancer, and Ron, an accountant. Kylie inherited her looks, blue eyes, wide smile and pop's most photographed legs, from her Welsh mother. Both are exactly the same height, a millimetre or so over five feet. Between Kylie and sister Dannii was a brother, Brendan, who also works in London, but for an Australian TV company. They grew up in the affluent eastern suburbs of Melbourne.

Emulating her little sister was what drove the teenage Kylie to answer a press advert wanting young actors for a TV drama, The Henderson Kids. She had already had a couple of small parts on TV, but nothing to approach the fame of her younger sister Dannii, who was a national TV child star in Australia. Even now one of Kylie's websites – though perhaps these days with a hint of irony – is called 'Dannii's Sister'. Dannii, too, was later to become a pop star in Britain, though over here big sister has ruled the roost. The TV director Chris Langman, who cast Kylie in The Henderson Kids, has recalled: 'She was vulnerable and very shy, and it came across. At the time, Kylie was living in the shadow of her sister, Dannii. I think she found that hard, but it's possible to be shy, yet driven, and that was Kylie.' . . .

In 1987 Pete Waterman was approached by someone from Mushroom Records in Australia. They had just signed Kylie Minogue and wanted Waterman to loan them an engineer to help them get the Stock Aitken Waterman high-energy sound. Waterman sent Mike Duffy, who got Kylie to do a version of 'The Locomotion'. It went to number one, and Duffy advised Waterman to take the girl on full time. Waterman had never heard of Kylie Minogue. He had never watched Neighbours. He said he would take her on and then promptly forgot about it. A few weeks later he got a call from Mike Stock saying there was 'a small Antipodean in reception expecting to do something with us now'. Waterman retorted: 'She should be so lucky' – which Stock immediately thought sounded like a song. And he started writing the lyrics. Yes, it really does sound like one of 'those' pop stories. But the parties concerned maintain it is true. 'I Should Be So Lucky' became Kylie's first British number one. The future Pop Idol judge began to realise he might have chanced on something special. Her debut album sold 14 million copies.

Text B Factual panel

Born:	Kylie Ann Minogue, Melbourne, Australia, 28 May 1968.
Parents:	Ron (an accountant) and Carol (whose family migrated from Wales in 1955).
Family:	Younger brother Brendan; younger sister Dannii.
School:	Camberwell High, Melbourne.
TV career:	First role, at the age of 12, in *The Henderson Kids*, followed by *The Sullivans* and *Skyways*; joined *Neighbours* in 1985; appeared in 542 episodes before leaving in 1988.
Singles:	'I Should Be so Lucky'; 'The Locomotion'; 'Especially for You' (with Jason Donovan); 'Got to Be Certain'; 'Je Ne Sais Pas Pourquoi'; 'Hand on Your Heart'; 'Never too Late'; 'Tears on My Pillow'; 'Confide in Me'; 'Where the Wild Roses Grow' (with Nick Cave); 'Spinning Around'; 'Can't Get You out of My Head'; 'In Your Eyes'.
Albums:	Kylie (1988); Enjoy Yourself (1989); Rhythm of Love (1990); Kylie Minogue (1994); Light Years (2000); Fever (2001); Confide in Me (2001).
Films:	*The Delinquents* (1989); *Streetfighter* (1994); *Moulin Rouge* (2001).
Business:	Her company Kaydeebee owns the rights to all her music; she launched the Love Kylie underwear range last year.
Awards:	Australian TV Logie award for best actress (1986); best international female singer and best international album at the Brits 2002.
Autobiography:	*Kylie*.
Worth:	Approximately £13m.
Likes:	Flake chocolate bars, flowers and Thai food.
Dislikes:	Brussels sprouts, snails and rudeness.
She says:	'When I donned the hot pants, I didn't expect that two years later it would be getting such attention.'
They say:	'From the first, I thought there was something about her, and if you could bottle it, you'd be a billionaire' – Pete Waterman.

Activity 2 Comparing the texts

1 What do you learn from text A that you couldn't really learn from text B?
2 Which text is more entertaining to read?
3 What are the advantages of presenting information in sentences and paragraphs, as in text A?
4 What are the advantages of using lists as in text B?
5 Why do you think the newspaper uses both types of text side-by-side?

Activity 3   A writing challenge

Imagine you have been asked to inform readers about the life of a famous writer, Charles Dickens.

Read this fact-file about Dickens.

Charles Dickens fact-file

Full name:	Charles John Huffham Dickens.
Born:	1812.
Died:	1870.
Father:	Clerk in Navy pay office, then imprisoned for being in debt.
Background:	Worked in blacking warehouse aged 12.
Early job:	Reporter in the House of Commons for *The Morning Chronicle*.
Career:	Approached by Chapman & Hall to write a book.
First novel:	*The Pickwick Papers* (1836–7), published in 20 sections.
Other writing:	Many popular novels, such as *Nicholas Nickleby*, *David Copperfield*, *Great Expectations*.
Home life:	Married to Catherine. Large family of eight children. Separated in 1858.

1   Imagine you are producing a leaflet for readers aged 11–14. The aim is to get them interested in Dickens' life and works.

What would you need that this fact-file does not provide?

Think about:
- Quotations (from what? About what?)
- Opinions (from whom? About what?)
- Other information (such as?)
- Pictures (of what?)

Brainstorm the materials and information you would need for an effective leaflet.

2   Imagine you have been asked to write the biography of Charles Dickens. A biography is the story of someone's life.

Talking point

Where would you begin?

Now look at this comment from Caroline Radcliff, someone who studies biographies:

In the light of her comment, can you think of a different way of starting the biography?

'The trouble with biographies is that they often start with the person's birth and end with their death. This can be very boring and predictable for the reader. The best biographers think of other ways of hooking the reader's interest.'

3 Look at these two openings of biographies about Dickens. One was written by Dickens' friend, John Forster. The other was written by the novelist and biographer, Peter Ackroyd.

Compare the way they both begin their writing.

Text A Forster

CHARLES DICKENS, the most popular novelist of the century, and one of the greatest humorists that England has produced, was born at Lanport, in Portsea, on Friday, the seventh of February, 1812. His father, John Dickens, a clerk in the Navy pay office, was at this time stationed in the Portsmouth Dockyard.

Text B Ackroyd

CHARLES DICKENS was dead. He lay on a narrow green sofa – but there was room enough for him, so spare had he become – in the dining room of Gad's Hill Place. He had died in the house which he had first seen as a small boy and which his father had pointed out to him as a suitable object of his ambitions; so great was his father's hold upon his life that, forty years later, he had bought it. Now he had gone.

4 Look at the statements below. Which text does each statement best apply to?

	Applies to text A	Applies to text B	Applies to neither
Statement a)			
Statement b)			

Try to explain why. Structure your response like this:

This statement best applies to _____ because _____ .

a) This text is the most obvious way of writing a biography. It starts at the beginning of the writer's life.
b) This text is aimed at people who already know a lot about the writer.
c) This text sounds more like a novel than a non-fiction text.
d) This text helps us to visualize (believe we can see) the scene.

e) This text tells us about the writer's own attitude to Dickens.

f) This text would make me want to read on.

g) This text feels very authoritative (trustworthy).

h) This text seems designed to entertain more than inform.

i) This text is very dull.

j) This text is easy to read.

k) This text has a clear target audience, which is ....

Task

Writing a mini-biography

Work with a partner, imagining that he or she is famous for something. You have been asked to write the opening section of a biography about your partner to appear in a newspaper. Your task is to find out information about your partner, to make it interesting to an audience who don't already know much about him or her, and to write the first 250 words.

You will need to approach this in three parts:

Stage 1: Researching the information

Plan some questions or use a questionnaire which will help you quickly to find out information about your subject.

Think of questions about his or her:

♦ background
♦ early life
♦ achievements
♦ hopes and fears

Think about how to write this information down:

♦ in random notes
♦ in a table or using boxes
♦ under key headings

Stage 2: Planning the writing

How will you make your mini-biography interesting?

How will you structure your writing?

Will you start at the beginning of your subject's life?

Will you instead start with a key moment which will hook the reader's interest?

Stage 3: Writing the biography

Experiment with some different styles:

a) Chronological (i.e. starting at the beginning)

Chloe Brown was born in Pakenham, Suffolk, in 1988. Her parents are Tom and Jayne . . .

b) Focusing on a key incident

> *Chloe Brown thought she was going to die in a small pond in North Wales. It had started as a family holiday outing . . .*

c) Start with a quotation

> *'"Never again." Chloe looks at me with an expression of determination. "Never again will I allow my brother to persuade me to go canoeing" . . .'*

LANGUAGE WORKSHOP

Exploring structure

Some texts need a chronological sequence – things being told in the order they take place. For example, recipes must be written in the right order, otherwise the cooking will go wrong.

Some explanation texts use chronological order, but start with a more general opening paragraph.

Look again at the extract from the profile of Kylie Minogue on pages 102–103. Below, we consider some more of this article. The opening sentences of a few main paragraphs in the profile are given.

Use the headings to explore how the writer has structured the piece. Write down what the topic is (e.g. Kylie now; Kylie's childhood; Kylie's ambitions, and so on). Then, look at the linking words, and try to explain how they help the reader to follow the text.

	Opening of paragraph	Topic	Linking words
A	It was a below-par BRIT awards this week . . .		this week
B	In case anyone watching was not aware that she is continually named 'rear of the year', she lifted the back of her dress above one cheek in the style of the tennis player on the Athena poster . . .		In case
C	After a year that also saw her play the Absinthe Fairy in the film *Moulin Rouge*, a new career opportunity now beckons . . .		After a year that
D	Kylie Ann Minogue was born 33 years ago in Melbourne . . .		33 years ago
E	In 1987 Pete Waterman was approached by someone . . .		In 1987
F	It was not just in her professional life that Kylie wanted new directions . . .		just
G	Besides, an automaton wouldn't have taken valuable years out of her career to reinvent herself . . .		Besides

WRITING TO EXPLAIN

Look at this list of features of explanation texts:

- they often start with a general statement
- they are written in chronological order
- they might use bullet points rather than sentences and paragraphs
- they might use diagrams or tables
- they might use imperative verbs in the present tense (i.e. commands, such as *lift the tin . . .*)
- each sentence might cover only one piece of information
- connectives are used which relate to the order of things happening (e.g. *next, then, later*)
- there is not much description, except where it will help the reader

Exploring audience

These texts require you to give information to your reader. You need therefore to think about your audience:

How well does he or she know me?

How much does he or she know about the topic?

Who am I writing for?

Does he or she just need the facts, or should I aim to entertain as well?

How straightforward should the language be?

Could I use layout features to communicate the information better?

Activity 4 Looking at audience

1 Imagine you are explaining how to use a new type of MP3 or DVD player. How would you present the information differently for:

- someone who has used MP3s/DVDs for several years?
- someone who has never owned a video or personal stereo?

For which audience would you:

- use more technical language?
- use pictures and diagrams?
- use lots of description?

2 A good example of the way writers need to think about the way they explain things is in recipes. Imagine you are writing a recipe for chocolate brownies (gooey slices of chocolate cake).

How would the audience affect the way you write the recipe? Look at the statements below and decide whether you would put them in column A, or column B, or both.

A	B
If the reader was an experienced cook . . .	If the reader was cooking brownies for the first time . . .

a) I would use a list of numbered points, or bullet points, rather than long paragraphs of description.
b) I would make sure there was a picture of the finished product.
c) I would use technical terms without needing to explain them.
d) I would want to address the reader directly ('You should now . . .' rather than 'Now mix this').

3 Look at these two recipes for brownies. One is from a Blue Peter Annual, the other from a cookery book by Delia Smith. Use the prompts below to explore the way the writers think about the audience.

Text A

Blue **Peter**
Chocolate Brownies

INGREDIENTS
100g butter
225g golden caster sugar
40g cocoa powder
2 eggs
1 teaspoon vanilla essence
50g self-raising flour
50g chocolate chips

Chocolate brownies are a must for any party. To make 12 to 16 delectable chocolate squares follow this easy recipe and your friends and family will be amazed at your culinary skills.

Method
Put the butter in a small pan and melt over a low heat. Take the pan off the heat and stir in the cocoa powder, making sure you remove any lumps.
Beat the eggs in a large bowl. Add the sugar and mix until smooth. Now put the cocoa mixture in the egg mixture and stir thoroughly before adding vanilla essence. Gradually add the self-raising flour through a sieve and keep stirring until it becomes a sticky mixture. Finally, add the chocolate chips.
Line a shallow square or oblong cake tin with greaseproof paper. Transfer the mixture to the tin and place in the middle of a preheated oven at 180° or gas mark 4 for around 30 minutes. The chocolate brownies will be crispy on top and gooey in the middle. Leave them in the tin for roughly 10 minutes before cutting into squares. Carefully transfer them to a cooling rack and wait until they are cool enough to eat.

Now simply enjoy!

Text B

American Brownies

4 oz butter (110 g)

2 oz American unsweetened chocolate (available at specialised food shops) or plain dessert chocolate (50 g)

2 eggs, beaten

8 oz granulated sugar (225 g)

2 oz plain flour (50 g), sifted

1 teaspoon baking powder

1/4 teaspoon salt

4 oz chopped nuts (110 g) – these can be walnuts, almonds, hazelnuts or Brazils or a mixture

(Makes 15 squares)

Brownies are squidgy, nutty chocolate bars; they are not cakes and therefore do not have the texture of a cake. They are supposed to be moist and chewy, but because of their moistness people tend to think they haven't cooked them long enough. So if this appeals to you, and you want to be really self-indulgent, here goes.

Pre-heat the oven to gas mark 4, 350°F (180°C).

An oblong tin measuring 7 x 11 inches (18 x 28 cm) well-greased and lined with grease-proof paper. Bring the paper up a good 2 inches (5 cm) above the rim of the tin.

First of all melt the butter and the chocolate (broken up into small pieces) together in the top of a double saucepan (or else place in a basin fitted over simmering water on a very low heat). Away from the heat, stir all the other ingredients into the butter and chocolate mixture thoroughly, then spread all this in the lined tin.

Bake in the oven for 30 minutes, until the mixture shows signs of shrinking away from the side of the tin, and the centre feels springy. A knife inserted in the centre should come out cleanly (but don't overcook - it will firm up as it cools). Then leave the mixture in the tin to cool for 10 minutes before dividing into approximately fifteen squares and transferring them to a wire rack to finish cooling.

Use this scale to answer the questions below on how much the reader knows about the topic:

1 —————— 2 —————— 3 —————— 4 —————— 5

Knows very little   Already knows a lot

Finish these statements:

a) In text A, the audience's current knowledge is around the number . . . . I can tell this because . . . .

b) In text B, the audience's current knowledge is around the number . . . . I can tell this because . . . .

WRITING TO DESCRIBE

Descriptive writing helps readers to visualize people and places.

Descriptive writing occurs in:

- novels, poetry, and short stories
- brochures for holidays, cars, and property
- essays about places
- reviews of films and concerts

Sometimes it is personal. Sometimes it is impersonal.

Activity 5 Using description

1 Look at this collection of texts which use descriptive writing. For each one try to work out what the text type is: fiction, non-fiction, review, brochure, essay, and so on.

A

Tucked into the folds of the Serra de Tramuntana on Mallorca's rugged north coast, the small resort of Cala Sant Vicenç must count as one of the island's most delightful corners.

B

It looks great. It makes the Audi TT – with which it partly shares a profile – seem about as classy as a pair of white stilettos. It has the softness and cuteness that Japanese sports cars tend to go in for, but without giving the impression – the way some Mazdas and Toyotas do – that what it really longed to be was a bumper car.

C

Light on; click. In the yellow bath of the bedside lamplight, she examined her left arm, holding up the limp, insensate sausage with her right hand. It interested her, how heavy just one little arm could become when the muscles inside it stopped working; even more interesting to realise how much work those muscles must be doing even when you thought they were relaxed.

D

The columns of smoke merged and became a monstrous curtain which blocked the sky ... There were fire hoses along the side of the road, climbing over one another like a helping of macaroni, with those sad little fountains spraying out from the leaks, as they always seem to do from all fire hoses.

2 Now look at the way the writers use description. Which texts . . .

a) are most and least descriptive (put them in order)

b) are most and least personal? This means that you feel the writer's own opinion. Which seems most detached? Put them in order.

3 Choose one of the texts. Re-write it with NO description at all. Make it as factual and undescriptive as you can. What did you have to do to the text to achieve this? Which words did you leave out or delete?

Activity 6 Describing places

One of the most common descriptive tasks that is set in the exam is to describe a place you know or can imagine. For example:

◆ **Describe** one of the following in such a way that it can easily be imagined by your reader: a city at night; a deserted beach; a busy shopping centre.

◆ Places can seem different at different times of the year. Choose one of the following places: a school playground; a High Street; a pond; a country lane. **Describe** it in winter and summer.

Talking point

Brainstorm what you think are the essential ingredients in doing well in this task.

1 Look at this example of descriptive writing by Gareth, a student in Year 10. The task was to write a description of a busy shopping centre. This is how he started off. How well do you think his descriptive writing works?

It is 3 pm on a Saturday afternoon and the shopping centre is really busy. There are lots of people around. The place is heaving. Some people are carrying bags. Others are standing around chatting or laughing. Most people seem happy but some people seem fed up.

Give Gareth's work a rating from 1 to 5:

1 ——————— 2 ——————— 3 ——————— 4 ——————— 5

Very boring   Very interesting

Complete this memo to Gareth, telling him how he could improve his work.

Memo to Gareth:

To improve this you need to . . . .

2   Now read these hints from Fozia Hussain, who teaches creative writing.

Hints on descriptive writing

- A good piece of descriptive writing uses as many of the senses as possible.
- Remember that you can be subjective or objective. This means that you might be giving your opinion (words to describe a dog might include judgement words such as *beautiful, friendly, adorable*); or you might be objective and factual (words might be *large, brown, furry*, and so on). Decide whether you are supposed to be involved or detached.
- You are aiming to help the reader to visualize a scene so use as many specific details as possible – the names of products, exact colours, similes to compare the place or person to something/someone else.
- Good descriptive writing isn't full of adjectives and adverbs. It uses well-chosen verbs and adverbs. For example: 'The man walked **slowly** down the road' might be expressed as 'Mr Williams **staggered** along the pavement'. 'Staggered' helps us to visualize the way he walks better than 'walked slowly'.
- Description very often relies on emotion to convey its point. Because of this, verbs, adverbs, and adjectives often convey more to the reader than do nouns.

Now take Gareth's description of a shopping centre and see how you can improve it.

◆ How will you create a strong visual picture?
◆ How will you use other senses?
◆ How will you make it more specific and less general?

Write your version and compare it with those of others in your group.

Activity 7 Building your reading skills

Look at this extract from Joanne Harris's novel *Chocolat*. In it, the narrator and her daughter have arrived in a small French village. Here she describes her first impressions. Use the questions which follow to explore the writer's use of description.

It's as good a place as any. Lansquenet-sous-Tannes, two hundred souls at most, no more than a blip on the fast road between Toulouse and Bordeaux. Blink once and it's gone. One main street, a double row of dun-coloured half-timbered houses leaning secretively together, a few laterals running parallel like the tines of a bent fork. A church, aggressively whitewashed, in a square of little shops. Farms scattered across the watchful land. Orchards, vineyards, strips of earth enclosed and regimented according to the strict apartheid of country farming: here apples, there kiwis, melons, endives beneath their black plastic shells, vines looking blighted and dead in the thin February sun but awaiting triumphant resurrection by March . . . Behind that, the Tannes, small tributary of the Garonne, fingers its way across the marshy pasture. And the people? They look much like all others we have known; a little pale perhaps in the unaccustomed sunlight, a little drab. Headscarves and berets are the colour of the hair beneath, brown, black or grey. Faces are lined like last summer's apples, eyes pushed into wrinkled flesh like marbles into old dough. A few children, flying colours of red and lime-green and yellow, seem like a different race. As the *char* advances ponderously along the street behind the old tractor which pulls it, a large woman with a square, unhappy face clutches a tartan coat about her shoulders and shouts something in the half-comprehensible local dialect; on the wagon a squat Santa Claus, out-of-season amongst the fairies and sirens and goblins, hurls sweets at the crowd with barely restrained aggression. An elderly small-featured man, wearing a felt hat rather than the round beret more common to the region, picks up the sad brown dog from between my legs with a look of polite apology. I see his thin graceful fingers moving in the dog's fur; the dog whines; the master's expression becomes complex with love, concern, guilt. No-one looks at us. We might as well be invisible; our clothing marks us as strangers, transients.

1   How many senses does the writer refer to? Can you find examples of:
    ◆ sight   ◆ sound   ◆ touch?

2   Pick out **two** examples of Joanne Harris's writing which you think powerfully describe the scene. Try to explain why you think they work well.

3   Are there any parts of her writing which you think are less successful? Again, say why.

1   How many senses does the writer refer to? Can you find examples of:
    ◆ sight   ◆ sound   ◆ touch?

2   The writer uses some similes to create her description. These are comparisons using the linking words *like* or *as*. Choose **one** example and say what you like or dislike about it.

3   Pick out **two** examples of Joanne Harris's writing which you think powerfully describe the scene. Comment on why her choice of language works especially well.

EXAM HINTS

◆ Remember to pick short quotations from the text. Place them in speech marks. Try to comment on specific words used by the writer in the quotation.

◆ Keep your style impersonal and detached unless you really want to emphasize your personal opinion: 'The writer creates a powerful feeling of . . .' rather than 'I think the writer creates . . .'.

◆ Leave a space between each answer to help the examiner follow your ideas easily and logically.

Activity 8   Building your writing skills

Everyday places can become disturbing at night. Choose one of the following settings and write a description of it by day and then by night:

◆ an old house   ◆ a school   ◆ a bus shelter

EXAM HINTS

◆ Brainstorm ideas first.

◆ Write down interesting words which will help you to evoke the right atmosphere.

◆ Think about your first sentence – how will you grab the reader's attention?

◆ How many different senses will you manage to include?

◆ How will you organize your writing into paragraphs?

◆ How personal will you make the writing? Or will you keep it entirely detached?

SAMPLE ANSWER

Writing a humorous description

A Year 10 class was asked to write a humorous description of their local town or village. Here Tom writes about his village in Suffolk.

How well do you think he uses description to capture the reader's attention and to entertain us? What feedback would you give him?

Tom's description	Comments by Examiner
On a small point on a map of Britain, in the south-east, in the middle of nowhere lies an unheard of, uninteresting and more often than not unseen village that goes by the name of Ixworth.	This is a good opening paragraph. It sets the scene well. Would it be better if it was a little shorter?
Already you may have an impression in your mind as to just how exhilarating the village is, but whatever you imagine is all false, the reality of things is worse than you can imagine and no matter how hard I try, words just won't be able to explain the sheer terror that inhabits this small village. When entering Ixworth, you are deprived of the real world and enter a place where you automatically feel unwanted and out of place. This is mainly due to the fact that 99% of Ixworth is occupied by people over the age of 60, who have lived there from their great great great granddad's day, and by now, have had 5 children who haven't visited for 30 years and don't intend to either as they've got more sense than their parents. They know what happens when you visit. It's simple really, you just come along, unaware of the signs put before you as you enter. You see road signs with messages such as 'Welcome to Ixworth'. This is what death is like printed in front of you, but you choose to ignore it until it is too late. You enter, just for a few hours, to see your parents who you haven't seen in a few years and instantaneously, you end up there for a few days, listening to the locals' constant jabbering on about how the teenagers shouldn't be allowed to hang around in parks and why computers have ruined the 20th century.	The way you introduce the reader as 'you' is good. It makes the style much more direct.
Before you know it, those few days have turned into weeks and as you struggle to leave, you no longer have the energy. This place is Ixworth.	Nice balance of a longer and then short sentence. This shows your ability to control language.
There is nothing to gain from living here. There are no rainbows hiding behind the clouds and there is no happy ending. It's just a nightmare, which appears never ending. Many things are lost when entering Ixworth. There have been a few robberies here and there and we all suspect there to be some form of an Old Age Pensioner Secret Society lurking somewhere, but the one thing that you created for yourself and is lost is hope. You suddenly begin to forget all of the things that are important and focus on escape. Your animal drives come into full function and everything is an isolated blur, which is made hazy due to the pain that you must suffer from living here. Here, being Ixworth.	Some good descriptive writing here, and some well-thought-out jokes.

Tom's description	Comments by Examiner
For a village, I suppose it isn't that bad. I mean, we've got the local shop, dentists, doctors, butchers, garage, police station and fire station. I mean, that can't be a bad thing, can it? Wrong. You've got a bunch of over-aged, over-weight and incompetent buffoons, trying to achieve a simple task, and failing miserably. The shop tends to sell more out-of-date stock than fresh. The police seem to sleep more than work and the firemen are never needed apart from when a corpse has to be carried out from a house and it's so heavy, the locals are unable.	The change to more positive points at this stage seems unexpected. Perhaps it needs an initial connective – such as 'On the other hand . . .'
I'm not sure if anyone is aware of a possible exit from Ixworth. If I were to rename it, then 'Village of the Damned' would be a perfect and more realistic title. We are all damned to a life of failure, like a curse in the air, it shall spread from person to person, leaving them in a job which just about pays the bills and gives them enough money to buy a pint at the local pub, every Friday. This one day will be me, as it is unstoppable, like a plague.	More comical moments.
If you'd be so kind to listen for a moment, I have some advice to offer you and it may be the best advice you ever hear. Stay well clear, of Ixworth.	The ending feels a bit flat. I can see that you want to pull the writing together but it needs more drama.

Conclusion

A good example of the way descriptive writing can help us to visualize places, even though this one is done negatively. Some of the jokes work well. Some paragraphs are a bit long and some of the points feel a bit repetitive.

Work likely to be produced by a B+ grade candidate.

QUICK ACTIVITIES FOR ENGLISH

These quick activities are designed to help you prepare for the requirements of English papers 1 and 2. The emphasis is on developing your knowledge of what is required in the exams, and your reading and writing skills. They should be done in a quick, focused way at the start or end of a lesson and last no more than ten minutes.

HOW TO USE THEM FOR MAXIMUM IMPACT

♦ Use them at the start of a lesson in the final run-up to your exams – i.e. the last few lessons of your English course.

♦ Keep them fast-paced. Don't let them run over ten minutes.

♦ Where possible, work with someone else and keep reflecting on *how* you are approaching a task, as well as on what you are doing.

♦ They are chiefly tasks to get you thinking, planning, and reflecting. You are not expected to produce polished work.

♦ Keep focused throughout – ten minutes of concentrated skills work now will really pay off in the final exam.

Quick activity 1 Knowing the exam requirements
Working in pairs or small groups . . .

Look at these facts about your GCSE English and English Literature exams. At the moment they are presented in a very boring format.

Your ten-minute task is to choose the key points and draft a poster which gives students the essential information they need to know about either the English *or* English Literature exam. Help your readers to see at a glance what they need to know and do for each section of each paper.

Make it visual, easy to understand and memorable.

English

Paper 1 is worth 30% of the marks. Paper 2 is worth 30% of the marks. Coursework is worth 40% of the marks. Paper 1 lasts $1\frac{3}{4}$ hours. Paper 2 lasts $1\frac{1}{2}$ hours. Paper 1 has two sections. Paper 2 has two sections. The two sections in paper 1 are: Reading non-fiction and media texts, and Writing to argue/persuade/advise. The two sections in paper 2 are: Poetry from different cultures and traditions, and Writing to inform/explain/describe.

English Literature

English Literature has just one paper. It is worth 70% of your final grade. The other 30% of your grade comes from coursework. The paper lasts $1\frac{3}{4}$ hours. There are two sections. Section A is post-1914 prose. Section B is a poetry question using the *Anthology*.

Quick activity 2   English exam requirements quiz

Test your knowledge of the English exam. Work on your own or in pairs and write down quick answers to these questions:

English

For English there are ____ exam papers
Paper 1 lasts ____ hours
On paper 1 there are two sections. Section A is about . . .
Section B is about . . .
Paper 2 lasts ____ hours
There are two sections. Section A is about . . .
Section B is about . . .
Overall, these two exams are worth _____ of my final English grade

Quick activity 3   English Literature exam requirements quiz

Test your knowledge of the English Literature exam. Work on your own or in pairs and write down quick answers to these questions:

English Literature

The English Literature paper is worth ____ of my overall English Literature grade
It lasts ____ hours
The text I will need to know well for section A is . . .
For section B I will need to know . . .
I will need to take these texts into the exam . . .

Quick activity 4   Response to text types

In English paper 1, you will need to respond to an unseen non-fiction or media text. Build your skills in spotting key features of texts. Read the text on the next page and spend three minutes working out:

- What is this text about?
- What kind of person wrote it?
- What is its purpose (to persuade? inform? entertain?)
- What type of text is it, and how can you tell?

It was on a bright day of midwinter, in New York. The little girl who eventually became me, but as yet was neither me nor anybody else in particular, but merely a soft anonymous morsel of humanity – this little girl, who bore my name, was going for a walk with her father. The episode is literally the first thing I can remember about her, and therefore I date the birth of her humanity from that day.

Quick activity 5   Response to text types

In English paper 1, you will need to respond to an unseen non-fiction or media text. Build your skills in spotting key features of texts. Read the text below and spend three minutes working out:

- What is this text about?
- What kind of person wrote it?
- What is its purpose (to persuade? inform? entertain?)
- What type of text is it, and how can you tell?

Urquhart castle is probably one of the most picturesquely situated castles in the Scottish Highlands. Located 16 miles south-west of Inverness, the castle, one of the largest in Scotland, overlooks much of Loch Ness. Visitors come to stroll through the ruins of the 13th-century castle because Urquhart has earned the reputation of being one of the best spots for sighting Loch Ness's most famous inhabitant.

Quick activity 6   Response to text types

In English paper 1, you will need to respond to an unseen non-fiction or media text. Build your skills in spotting key features of texts. Read the text on the next page and spend three minutes working out:

- What is this text about?
- What kind of person wrote it?
- What is its purpose (to persuade? inform? entertain?)
- What type of text is it, and how can you tell?

Yannaki was that stock Greek village character, the traveller come home after experiencing glamorous doings and glorious events in far-off places. True to type, he spoke a little Anglo-American and, more uncommonly, a little French; he was always on hand to help out if foreigners came to the village. He seemed a kind and cheerful man, rich too; at any rate, he owned a spare donkey and was prepared to lend me this animal, along with a boy to talk to it, so that I could ride into the town when I needed to stock up with fresh supplies of beans and oil, bottled wine, cheese, dried fruit, and boxes of the delicious Turkish Delight which was – still is – a speciality of the island.

For days I scanned the horizon for sight of an English yacht. I could, in my turn, have bartered fresh vegetables and fruit for the jars of mustard pickles which I knew must grace the table of any English 'lordos' grand enough to be roaming the Aegean seas. It was late in the season. That way no yacht came.

Quick activity 7 Response to text types

In English paper 1, you will need to respond to an unseen non-fiction or media text. Build your skills in spotting key features of texts. Read the text below and spend three minutes working out:

- What is this text about?
- What kind of person wrote it?
- What is its purpose (to persuade? inform? entertain?)
- What type of text is it, and how can you tell?

Wright had Klinsmann under wraps; Waddle released Parker, Beardsley went through once, and then again . . . Hassler took the German's first serious strike, and it deflected away from Pearce for their first corner – but Butcher towered up, and headed away. Then Wright picked a through ball off Klinsmann's feet; the German looked angry and rattled. You could feel their pace, their threat – but still we had them, and the first phase was all England.

No question: England could win this.

The press box was buzzing. Gazza tangled with Brehme; he got another shot in, then broke to the left corner, won a free-kick . . .

Let's all have a disco
Let's all have a disco.

It was more than a disco, it was history.

Quick activity 8 Response to text types

In English paper 1, you will need to respond to an unseen non-fiction or media text. Build your skills in spotting key features of texts. Read the text below and spend three minutes working out:

- ◆ What is this text about?
- ◆ What kind of person wrote it?
- ◆ What is its purpose (to persuade? inform? entertain?)
- ◆ What type of text is it, and how can you tell?

Though I ran and ran as I have never run in my life before, and my heart pounded in my ears and my lungs stiffened with the pain of drawing breath, time went suddenly into slow motion. Each step was weighted with lead; I wanted to fly over the ground and, as in some horrid nightmare, I felt as though I were scarcely moving.

The rhino were swiftly gaining upon me; their furious snorts overtook me on the wings of the gale. The boys, on the other hand, had disappeared as though the earth had swallowed them. I made one more desperate spurt and then, as I realised the utter futility of it, a fold in the hillside opened to receive me also. I tumbled headlong down a little cliff and landed on a ledge of heather.

Quick activity 9 Response to text types

In English paper 1, you will need to respond to an unseen non-fiction or media text. Build your skills in spotting key features of texts. Read the text below and spend three minutes working out:

- ◆ What is this text about?
- ◆ What kind of person wrote it?
- ◆ What is its purpose (to persuade? inform? entertain?)
- ◆ What type of text is it, and how can you tell?

The blacking warehouse was the last house on the left-hand side of the way, at old Hungerford-stairs. It was a crazy, tumble-down old house, abutting of course on the river, and literally overrun with rats. Its wainscotted rooms, and its rotten floors and staircase, and the old grey rats swarming down in the cellars, and the sound of their squeaking and scuffling coming up the stairs at all times, and the dirt and decay of the place, rise up visibly before me, as if I were there again. The counting-house was on the first floor, looking over the coalbarges and the river. There was a recess in it, in which I was to sit and work. My work was to cover the pots of paste-blacking; first with a piece of oil-paper, and then with a piece of blue paper; to tie them round with a string; and then to clip the paper close and neat, all round, until it looked as smart as a pot of ointment from an apothecary's shop.

Quick activity 10 Exploring mystery text types

Here are three extracts from different texts.

- What are they?
- What is their purpose?
- Who are they aimed at?
- How can you tell?

Text A

Freshly squeeze 2 oranges and pour the juice into a jug. Purée the flesh of 1 mango and pour into the jug with the orange juice. Whisk in 100ml natural yoghurt and a 15ml spoon honey, thoroughly. Pour into tall glasses over ice and serve.

Text B

Seville is voluptuous and evocative. It has to be seen, tasted and touched. The old quarter is Seville as it was and is. Walk in its narrow cobbled streets, with cascades of geraniums tumbling from balconies and the past shouts so loudly that one can almost glimpse dark-cloaked figures disappearing silently through carved portals.

Text C

The blood vessels of the circulatory system, branching into multitudes of very fine tubes (capillaries), supply all parts of the muscles and organs with blood, which carries oxygen and food necessary for life.

Quick activity 11 Exploring mystery text types

Here are three extracts from different texts.

- What are they?
- What is their purpose?
- Who are they aimed at?
- How can you tell?

Text A

Thirty years ago, Neil Armstrong was preparing for the most momentous step made by a human being in the twentieth century. But first he had to get there, wiggling his way out of the lunar module that had brought him and Aldrin this far.

Text B

Proud mum in a million Natalie Brown hugged her beautiful baby daughter Casey yesterday and said: 'She's my double miracle.'

Text C

Nutritionists recommend that adults include 18g of fibre in their diet each day. One typical bowl of Crunchy Bran delivers half of that amount in one go. And getting the other half of the fibre we need doesn't have to be hard work either.

Quick activity 12 Writing to argue, persuade, or advise

Some people think school uniform is a waste of time. Other people say it helps students to feel proud about their school.

You have been asked to write a letter to your Headteacher asking that the uniform policy is changed.

1 Brainstorm what you will say.
2 Think of the order of your points.
3 Write the opening paragraph.

Compare your work with a friend's.

Quick activity 13 Writing to argue, persuade, or advise

'Human beings can live healthily without eating meat. The way animals are treated is often disgusting.'

Write a leaflet encouraging readers to give up eating meat.

1 Brainstorm what arguments you might use.
2 Draft what a leaflet might look like.
3 Write a headline and one paragraph.

Compare your work with a friend's.

Quick activity 14 Writing to argue, persuade, or advise

Here is the opening of two students' responses to this question:

'Write a letter to your local council arguing for more facilities for young people.'

Text A

Dear Sir

We young people have not got enough facilities and we need more. There is hardly anything to do around here and we would like to have things like skateparks . . .

Text B

> *Dear Sir*
>
> *I would like to set up a meeting with you and some of my friends to discuss the possibility of developing facilities for young people in this area. We currently feel frustrated that there is very little for us to do . . .*

- ◆ What differences do you notice in the two letters?
- ◆ What advice would you give to each student on how to further improve their work?

Quick activity 15 Writing to inform, explain, or describe

Your school has been chosen as the centre for a major education conference. You have been asked to draft some details telling guests about the school.

Put together an information sheet telling them what they need to know.

- ◆ What information will you include?
- ◆ How will you organize it?
- ◆ Write a sample paragraph.
- ◆ Compare it with a friend's.

Quick activity 16 Writing to inform, explain, or describe

Choose one topic.

> Write a detailed description of a dangerous place you have visited.
>
> Write a description of a place you particularly like.
>
> Write a description of a busy town or city centre.
>
> Write a description of a deserted place – such as an empty beach.

- ◆ What would you describe?
- ◆ How would you organize your ideas?
- ◆ Write your first paragraph.

Quick activity 17 Writing to inform, explain, or describe

Here are two student responses to this question:

'You have been asked to help with a school training course for parents, showing them how to use the Internet. Write an instructional leaflet explaining to them the basics of using a web browser.'

Text A

A web browser like Internet Explorer lets you view pages on the Internet. When you first start the program it will go to the "home page". This is your starting-point for the Internet.

Text B

Internet Explorer is a Microsoft product that enables you to explore the Internet in a very straightforward way using a series of pages controlled by buttons. The main control you need to know about is the URL search window which is where you type in the address of the site you want to look at or, if you don't know the full site address, you could use a search engine like Google or Yahoo.

- ◆ What are the differences in the two texts?
- ◆ What advice would you give to each student?

EXAMINATION PRACTICE

This section is designed to help you build up the essential skills you will need for the final exams in English and English Literature. It gives you guidance on:

- Ten hints for successful revision
- Reading non-fiction and media texts
- Writing in exam conditions
- Improving your grade

TEN HINTS FOR SUCCESSFUL REVISION

1 Know that nothing is fixed.

Whatever your predicted grade, there is always room to do even better. Just as athletes push their bodies to superb success through coaching and training, so you can do the same with your brain. Treat the exams as you would an important race or swimming gala. Train for them. Feed and water your brain (your brain needs food, water and rest to function at its best).

2 Plan for success.

Put together a really systematic revision programme that allows you to work in sensible, short blocks of time (your maximum concentration time for any activity is unlikely to be more than 20 minutes).

3 Have your plan on the wall in the room where you work.

Use it to tick off or block out areas you have covered. This will help you to see that you are making progress.

4 Re-read your set texts actively.

Don't just read them. Keep notes on your thoughts and observations, and jot down useful quotations as you re-read. This will help you to organize your thoughts and ideas.

5 Find ways of motivating yourself.

If you find it really hard to revise, build rewards into your routine. For example, after three 20-minute revision sessions, allow yourself some time with a computer game or phoning a friend, or to have a drink. Choose whatever reward system will help you to get motivated.

6 Use your own learning style.

Some people learn visually. They like to use charts, pictures, words, colours, highlighter pens.

Others learn in an auditory way. They like to hear information. Read information aloud and tape it. Get someone to test you orally. Use music to help fix key ideas in your mind.

Some people learn by doing things – they need to make revision active. Study different topics in different rooms (this will help you to recall them). Copy key ideas onto strips of paper. Cut them up, shuffle them around and test yourself. Do anything that will make your learning active.

7 Revise your spellings.

Spelling is not the most important skill in your English exams but you need to be reasonably accurate. Keep a list of words that you consistently misspell (perhaps words like *because/necessary/separate*), and use the list to test yourself for one minute every day.

8 Practise using sentence variety.

The best writing has a range of sentences – short and long; simple, compound and complex. Practise writing paragraphs that use this range. For example, write a paragraph about any topic, starting and ending with a simple sentence. In the middle of the paragraph, use compound and complex sentences. Read it back to check how clear it is.

> Revision is not easy. Although everyone hates the thought of revising, some people manage to build a routine for themselves. Other people lose confidence and sometimes give up. However, revision is essential for exam success.

Start and end with simple sentences   **Complex and compound sentences**

9 Remember connectives.

Connectives help to indicate the 'direction' of a text to your reader. They are especially important in good non-fiction writing. Connectives you might use include:

however	*although*	*despite*
similarly	*on the other hand*	*therefore*
whenever	*because*	*in addition*
finally		

10 Don't believe everything you hear.

Some students will boast that they aren't bothering to revise. Ignore them. *You* are the most important person in this process. Very few people can do well in an exam without revision, so choose the times that suit you (such as early mornings or evenings) and plan your revision schedule.

READING NON-FICTION AND MEDIA TEXTS

Look at these five hints.

1 Use all the clues you can get.

Before you start reading, look at the layout of the text. Look for:

- headlines
- columns
- images
- questions
- boxes
- other text styles (e.g. bullet points)

The more you can tune in to the conventions of the text, the quicker you will absorb it.

2 Read actively.

Use a pencil to highlight key words or to make quick notes in the margin. These will help you to organize your ideas.

3 Look carefully at the question.

What are you being asked to do?

- spot information?
- give an opinion?
- re-write the text in a different form?

Understanding the question will be essential to the success of your answer, so underline the key words in the question.

4 Look out for connectives.

These will help you to follow the writer's thoughts or argument. You might underline or circle them as you read. Connectives will help you to understand the overall shape of the text. For example:

- *On the other hand / however*: the writer is balancing an opposing argument
- *Because / therefore*: the writer is giving a reason.

5 Pay close attention to the language.

For the best grades at GCSE you need to do much more than describe what a text is about. You need to show that you can comment on the writer's use of language. This means that you might say something about:

- **Structure** – how the text is organized. Is it in chronological order, or does it have a different structure? What does this tell the reader?
- **Sentences** – are different types used (simple, compound, complex), and what is their effect? Are the sentences mostly statements, or questions, or commands? Why? What is their effect?
- **Words** – are they familiar, unusual, poetic, descriptive, technical, emotive? Why has the writer chosen them?

Remember: don't just spot a feature of language, but try to explain the effect it has in this text.

Look at this table for some examples.

Language	Effect
Shakespeare has a character use the word 'butcher' about Macbeth.	This immediately emphasizes the brutality of Macbeth. It associates him with someone who slaughters animals. It makes the audience recognize the ruthless nature of Macbeth because he will stop at nothing.
The headline in an article about school meals uses the word 'crisis'.	This is an emotive term – it aims to get an emotional response from the reader. It makes the situation sound dramatic. The writer might have used a word like 'problem', 'confusion', or 'uncertainty', but instead he or she has chosen a word with much more emotional impact. In the context of the story, the word is an exaggeration.

WRITING IN EXAM CONDITIONS

Look at these five hints.

1   Exams aren't coursework.

The English course gives you plenty of opportunity to develop your style and to improve your accuracy. Coursework is important for writing practice and to express yourself. But the skills you need in exam conditions are different – you won't have time for drafting and re-drafting. You'll need to be able to plan and write without using a dictionary or thesaurus. Treat exam writing as something different from coursework, and prepare for it through regular practice. Some ideas are suggested below.

2 Practise planning.

To do well in the English and English Literature exams you need to be able to plan your answers. Structure is important. Spend time now finding which planning style best suits you.

Here are some possible examples:

- make a list of bullet points for ideas you want to include
- brainstorm a random list of ideas and then use arrows and notes to group them into the order you want
- use spider diagrams to begin with main ideas and group related ideas around them.

Practise planning using some of the exam-type questions in this book.

3 Practise writing.

Journalists are taught to capture their reader's attention from the first sentence. You need to do the same in an exam. You can't afford to write a boring or vague first sentence or paragraph. Practise writing opening paragraphs.

Look at these examples. They were written in response to the task:

Write a speech to persuade young people to become more aware of looking after the environment.

Example A	Example B	Example C
The environment is really important. Are you taking it for granted?	Perhaps you yawn any time someone uses a word like 'environment'. Beware. One day your yawn may become your last gasp for oxygen.	Question: which is the most selfish creature on the planet? Answer: the human being. The reason? . . .

Three Year 11 students wrote these responses in their mock exams. Which opening do you think works best? What advice would you give to each student?

4 Have a sense of style.

The best writing is usually clear and easy to understand. Getting high grades isn't a matter of writing the longest sentences and using the most difficult words. In fact, A and A* students usually use shorter sentences than grade B students. Their secret is sentence variety.

Look at these responses to the question:

What are the arguments for and against school uniform?

Example A: all simple sentences

> School uniform is irritating. It takes away people's freedom. It makes everyone look the same. It is boring and predictable. I don't like it.

Example B: all compound sentences

> School uniform is irritating and it takes away people's freedom. It makes everyone look the same and it is boring and predictable, and I don't like it.

Example C: all complex sentences

> School uniform, which makes everyone look the same, is boring and predictable. Because it takes away people's freedom, it causes huge irritation.

One secret of good writing is to vary your sentence structure to get a range of sentence types, like this:

> I dislike school uniform. I know that it is intended to look smart, but in practice it takes away people's individuality. Instead of making us feel proud of our school, too often it leaves us feeling irritated, even angry. It isn't good for our morale.

This is grade A writing because:

◆ it has sentence variety
◆ it uses interesting words which explain the writer's ideas well.

5   Avoid too much modification.

It can be tempting to add a lot of modification to your writing. This means using adjectives and adverbs to add description to nouns and verbs, like this:

The <u>unpleasant, bland, irritating</u> uniform   **modifying adjectives**
Which we are <u>always annoyingly</u> expected to wear   **modifying adverbs**

Too many modifiers can clog up your writing, so be brutal with yourself and choose exactly the words you need, rather than putting too many modifiers in each sentence.

IMPROVING YOUR GRADE

Here is a step-by-step guide to improving your grade in English and English Literature.

Current grade bracket	What you need to do to improve
G/F Reading: ◆ You respond to the main characters/events in a text Writing: ◆ You use straightforward vocabulary, and usually write in accurate basic sentences	Reading: Get to know the detail of texts more. Look at the way they are written. Try to say something about the writer's language. Writing: Spend time learning basic spellings. Vary your writing. Aim to use a range of sentences – short and long.
E/D Reading: ◆ You have a good basic understanding of texts ◆ You know the characters and storylines well ◆ You sometimes comment on the writer's choice of language Writing: ◆ Your spelling is generally accurate ◆ You plan stories well ◆ You use some interesting vocabulary	Reading: When writing about texts, give more specific examples to support your ideas. Use short rather than long quotations. Try to focus on the writer's exact choice of words and comment on their effect. Writing: Develop a bigger range of sentence structures. Use more short sentences, not just longer ones. Try to connect ideas without always using *and, but, or, then*. Pause to think of more interesting words and images in your writing.
C/B Reading: ◆ You understand texts well ◆ You show a good personal response ◆ You show an ability to discuss a writer's use of language Writing: ◆ Your writing is well controlled ◆ You have a good grasp of paragraphing, and can write well for different audiences	Reading: Look beneath the surface of texts. Look for hints about the way characters behave (e.g. what their choice of words reveals about them) and about writers' opinions. Focus on specific words and spend more time in your answers exploring the implications of these. Writing: Use a varied style. Try to surprise and entertain the reader with well-chosen, thoughtful word choices and a range of sentence styles. Use punctuation that helps you to balance thoughts and ideas – semi-colons and colons.
A/A* Reading: ◆ Your understanding of texts is very good and you comment on language features in an assured way Writing: ◆ You can write in a range of styles, very accurately, using a variety of impressive vocabulary	Reading: Extend the range of your reading by choosing a wider variety of reading material at home. Explore complex texts. Look at the way different writers (from journalists to travel writers to novelists) use vocabulary and sentence structures. Keep quotations short and frequent throughout your literature responses. Writing: Be experimental. Choose words that help the reader to visualize your ideas. Don't be afraid of using very short sentences when appropriate. Use a range of punctuation.

TOP GRADE COACHING

If you are aiming for an A or A* in English, these comments and activities are designed for you. They cover a range of reading and writing skills you will need to demonstrate in your final examinations. The activities are not simply sample questions or tasks. Instead, they are designed to help you learn what you need to do for the top grades. They are therefore small-scale, step-by-step demonstrations of advanced skills.

What do you need to know and do to gain an A or A*?

Reading

A

- Appreciate different possible interpretations
- Develop ideas
- Refer in detail to the language
- Skilfully compare texts.

A*

- Write high-level responses to texts, evaluating alternative and original interpretations
- Demonstrate flair and precision in developing ideas
- Make subtle, discriminating comparisons within and between texts.

Writing

A

- Shape and control writing in a range of styles
- Use a wide range of grammatical constructions, and well-constructed paragraphs
- Use ambitious and accurate vocabulary and punctuation.

A*

- Skilfully control writing and suit it to the purpose
- Use a wide vocabulary, precise fluent style, almost faultless spelling and punctuation.

English Literature

A

- Explore texts critically and sensitively
- Pay close attention to the writer's use of language
- Respond in a variety of forms
- Show awareness of the historical and cultural contexts of texts.

A*

- Show an enthusiastic personal response and give a sophisticated interpretation
- Communicate with flair in a range of forms
- Show originality in your analysis of texts and their contexts.

Reading non-fiction

You need to be able to read, understand, and interpret these texts. Making connections and comparisons will also be important.

Look again at this paragraph from Fergal Keane's autobiographical article about Christmas, which appeared on page 11. Some of the key language choices have been highlighted.

Now that I must **shepherd** a five-year-old boy through Christmas I am caught up again in the **whirling energy** of downtown streets, overseeing the writing of a letter to the North Pole and counting the days to a morning of gifts and bacon sandwiches. These last have been a family ritual **since time began**. As a child I used to wake around four o'clock on Christmas morning. My own son has **inherited** the habit. This Christmas I will sit down to lunch with 17 people in a house in County Clare. I have no doubt it will be chaotic. **Red-faced and overtired children** will first play and then do battle. When I say that they range in age from six months to 14 years you may be tempted to sympathise, or at least murmur: 'Thank God it's not me.'

Developing a response to the language

1   What would you say about the words that have been highlighted?
2   Why do you think they have been highlighted?
3   Are they the most interesting language features – the ones you would have identified?

What to say about language features

What would you need to say about the language to gain an A or A*?
Look at this sample sentence from a student likely to achieve grade B:

The writer uses the word 'shepherd' and this shows that he feels responsible for his son.

♦ What should the student say differently to gain an A or A*?

Look at this rewritten version:

Fergal Keane talks of his duty to 'shepherd' his son through Christmas. The word 'shepherd' emphasizes the strong sense of responsibility he feels as a father. It also suggests that he is perhaps protecting and guiding his child in a complicated world.

♦ How has the student developed her point?
♦ Is it more detailed?
♦ Is it better expressed?

Examiner's comment:

This shows a good attention to the language of the text, and the student explores the implications of the phrasing well. If the rest of the response were at a similar level, this could gain a grade A.

◆ What would an A* answer look like?

Fergal Keane uses the verb 'shepherd', which is appropriate given that the theme is Christmas. The word emphasizes the powerful sense of responsibility and duty the father feels for his child, and the role he plays in guiding his son through the Christmas season. The language also perhaps suggests that Fergal Keane will see Christmas afresh because he will relive his own childhood memories through his son's eyes.

Examiner's comment:

Notice the relish for language here – the way the student focuses on the specific details of the extract, drawing out ideas and implications. This is exceptional work.

Choose one or two of the other highlighted words in the extract and practise writing top grade comments which focus on the specific implications of the language.

Reading media texts

As you know, media texts include articles, leaflets, and scripts. For a top grade, you will need to show an understanding of:

◆ how the text approaches its audience
◆ how it is organized
◆ meanings and implications
◆ language features.

Look again at this part of the newspaper article which appeared on page 23, and focus in particular on the highlighted connectives.

A 15-month-old boy had to be rescued by fire officers after he accidentally locked himself in a bathroom.

Travis Tyler, of Kirkstead Road, Bury St Edmunds, was playing a game with his mother Tracey at just after 9.30am on Saturday **when** he ran into the bathroom and closed the door.

When Tracey tried to open the door **minutes later** she discovered that Travis had slipped the bolt, making it impossible for him to get out.

After she failed to open the door herself, Tracey called the fire brigade and Bury's Red Watch were on the scene within minutes.

Fire officers **then** set about getting the bathroom door open to free the mischievous youngster as quickly as possible.

135

Developing a response to the language

1   What would you say about the way the text is organized?
2   How is the writer using connectives to organize the writing?
3   Why are the paragraphs so short?
4   In what ways is the text typical of most newspaper articles?

What to say about language features

What would you need to say about the language to gain an A or A*?
Look at this sample sentence from a student likely to achieve grade B:

The writer uses connectives like 'when' and 'later' to link
ideas together in chronological order.

- What should the student say differently to gain an A or A*?

Look at this rewritten version:

The writer's use of connectives helps to structure the story in a
chronological sequence. The connectives are all words and
phrases that help to show when events took place, such as
'after', 'when', 'later', 'then'. This makes it easy for the reader
to follow the storyline in the correct order.

- How has the student developed her point?
- Is it more detailed?
- Is it better expressed?

Examiner's comment:

This comment is a good one because it makes a detailed reference to
the language and explains how the writer has structured the article. If
this level is sustained in the rest of the response, the student could gain
a grade A.

What would an A* answer look like?

The article starts with a topic sentence. This answers the
questions 'who', 'where' and 'what'. Unusually for a
newspaper article, it does not tell us 'when'. The aim of a topic
sentence is to gain our interest in the whole story, before then
giving a more detailed account of events. The subsequent
paragraphs give us that information, linking ideas together
using temporal connectives such as 'then', 'after' and 'later'.
This helps the reader to follow the sequence of events that led to
the child being released from the bathroom.

Examiner's comment:

This is an assured answer which shows a strong grasp of the way the text is structured. The student uses appropriate technical terms to explain the way the article has been organized. It is an extremely good answer.

Look at the avalanche article on page 21 and write a paragraph about the way the writer structures the article. Refer to some of the language features in detail.

Final hints on Reading tasks

- The Reading section is only an hour long and contains a lot for you to read. Be prepared for this.
- In preparation for the final exam, practise reading lots of texts in different styles – e.g. opening paragraphs from newspaper articles, magazines, leaflets. The more confident you can become in responding to unseen texts, the easier you will find the reading task.
- Remember that some texts will be media-based – think about the audience/purpose/style of the text.
- Tease out as many points as you can based on the language in the texts you read. Use short quotations and then comment in detail on the implications of the writer's use of words.

Post-1914 prose: *Lord of the Flies*

This paragraph was written by a student likely to achieve grade B. It is an answer to this question:

How important is the setting to the message of Lord of the Flies?

The setting is really important in the novel. For some of the characters the island is quite frightening – for example, the Littluns. For others it is a place of power – for example, Jack who paints his face and uses Castle Rock as the base for his supporters. This is a contrast to the start of the novel where in some ways the setting seems idyllic. It says: 'The shore was fledged with palm trees'.

- What advice would you give to improve this?
- How could it be organized differently?
- How could quotations be improved?
- Is there sufficient detail in each point?
- How could the style be improved?

Examiner's comments:

There are many good points in this paragraph. In fact, that is its main problem – it tries to cover too many too quickly. It needs a clearer structure. It needs more specific detail.

Next look at some opening sentences that would lead into a higher-level answer.

Sample A* openings:

1 From the outset, the mood of the island setting is a mixed one . . .
2 From the beginning of the novel, William Golding presents an ambivalent picture of the island . . .
3 The novel begins with the island described as a 'jungle'. There are 'thorns' and creepers. Within pages we read of a 'shore fledged with palm trees'. The setting is, in other words, a place of deeply mixed messages . . .

- Which of these openings do you like best – and why?
- Using one of the openings (if you wish), rewrite the sample student paragraph, aiming for a higher grade. Compare your version with someone else's.

Post-1914 prose: Of Mice and Men

Top grade students are able to respond to small details in the text, commenting on different possible interpretations and exploring the language used by the writer. Look at this extract from *Of Mice and Men*. It comes from the passage where Curley's wife is talking in the barn to Lennie.

> 'Coulda been in the movies, an' had nice clothes – all them nice clothes like they wear. An' I coulda sat in them big hotels, an' had pitchers took of me. When they had them previews I coulda went to them, an' spoke in the radio, an' it wouldn'ta cost me a cent because I was in the pitcher. An' all them nice clothes like they wear. Because this guy says I was a natural.' She looked up at Lennie, and she made a small grand gesture with her arm and hand to show that she could act. The fingers trailed after her leading wrist, and her little finger stuck out grandly from the rest.

Exploring the text

A top grade student will find a lot to say about this extract. Use these sentence starters to think of the different points you could make about the text:

1 Curley's wife keeps referring to the clothes she could have worn if she had made it in the movies. This shows that she is . . .

2 John Steinbeck shows an example of Curley's wife's acting style to show us that . . .

3 The extract shows that beneath the surface Curley's wife is . . .

4 By the end of this paragraph, we like Curley's wife more / less than before because . . .

5 The fact that her ideas are mostly connected by the conjunction 'and' suggests that . . .

Writing about the text

A student working towards grade B might say:

Curley's wife has ambitions to be an actress but the way she gestures shows us that actually she wouldn't be very good. She is really attracted to being a celebrity but does not appear to have the talent.

◆ What would you advise to improve this paragraph?

Think about:
◆ ideas   ◆ language   ◆ use of quotations.

Try re-writing the paragraph so that it is likely to gain a higher grade. Use one of these essay starters to get you under way. They are all taken from A and A* answers. Which do you think works best, and why?

A   Curley's wife continues to inhabit a world of broken promises and failed dreams . . .

B   Lennie is happy to sit and half-listen to Curley's wife. As readers we see beneath the surface of her character and recognize that . . .

C   Curley's wife's example of 'grand' acting says it all. It is a poignant demonstration of the way she deludes herself, attracted merely to the trappings of fame, but she is deeply talentless and doomed to fail . . .

Post-1914 prose: *The Catcher in the Rye*

This is a comment on Holden Caulfield from a student working towards grade C. What would you do to improve it?

Holden is quite a likeable character. He can be quite frustrating and even irritating though. At the start of the novel it takes quite a long time to understand him. He seems very big-headed and not very likeable. By the end we have begun to see much more about him, including his weaknesses.

139

◆ What do you like about this paragraph? What would you change?

Think about:
◆ the ideas   ◆ the structure and language
◆ the use of specific examples.

Try writing an improved version. Use these possible starters to get you under way. They are all taken from answers which gained A or A*. Which of these do you think works best, and why?

A   Holden is a complex and occasionally infuriating character . . .

B   Our response to Holden develops as we read the novel. At the outset he is . . .

C   From Holden's opening words, he makes a direct challenge to us ('If you really want to hear about it . . .') to read on. His personality captures our imagination and, as we begin to see his frailties revealed, we build a complex picture of what he is really like . . .

Writing to argue, persuade, and advise

Look at this sample from a letter written by a student who gained grade C. The task was:

Write an article for a local newspaper giving your opinion about zoos.

Zoos are cruel. How would you like to be cooped up all day in a cage with people gawping at you? It's not fair and I think that zoos should be closed down. Everyone has television these days so there's not even any need for people to visit zoos any more. Instead they can see everything they need to on TV.

1   What are the strengths and weaknesses of this opening paragraph?
2   Has the student adopted an appropriate style and approach to the audience?
3   How would you develop the writing to gain a grade A or A*?

Look at these sample starters. Each comes from the opening of an article written by a student who gained an A or A*.

Which do you think works best?

A   It is easy to judge zoos by what they used to be like, rather than by what they are today. The chief function these days of zoos is not displaying animals, but conservation.

B   The last time I went to London Zoo I was astonished that it was no longer an animal peep-show; instead it was a genuine, day-long learning experience, a journey into the amazing world of various creatures.

C   Imagine living in a cage all day. Just when you think things are all quiet you decide to take a rest. Then some screaming child lobs an ice-cream over the bars and there's nowhere to hide. Welcome to the reality of British zoos – homes not only for fabulous creatures, but also for degradation, cruelty and endless humiliation.

Using one of these if you wish, write your own opening paragraph on the topic of zoos.

Writing to inform, explain, and describe

Top grade candidates are skilful and choose their words carefully, knowing what style will best suit their audience.

Look at this example of a grade C description. It is written in response to this question:

Describe a difficult journey you have made.

When we went to Sardinia last year we were held up for a long time by a delay at Gatwick Airport and this made our journey very difficult. To make matters worse I had my younger sister with me. She is two. She didn't get much sleep and was really hard work as we waited in the departure lounge to find out what time we would be flying.

- What are the strengths and weaknesses of this description?
- How would you improve it?

Now look at these three alternative versions written by students who achieved A or A* grades. Look at:

- how they express the same ideas
- how they use language
- how they capture the reader's interest.

Which do you think works best, and why?

141

A   It felt as if we would spend our whole holiday at Gatwick. I got to know that departure lounge as if it was part of our own house. Shelley (my two-year-old sister) also treated it like home, screaming just as much as she usually does. This was not a good start to a difficult journey.

B   It ought to be easy. You turn up at the airport, you board the plane and you fly away to somewhere hot. Not today. We stayed somewhere hot – the departure lounge at Gatwick Airport – but we didn't fly away until six nerve-racking hours had been punctuated by my little sister Shelley's screams.

C   Sardinia shimmered beneath a broad, deep blue sky. The sun beat endlessly down and tourists baked slowly on the clear white beaches. I put the brochure down and looked around me. Shelley was screaming again, sitting on top of her Barbie knap-sack, and irritated faces looked at us from every part of the departure lounge. We were trying to go on holiday.

Final hints on Writing tasks

- Planning and sequencing are essential skills. Aim to write two sides as a maximum, not a minimum. Examiners will assess the quality, not the quantity of your writing.
- Remember the importance of getting the purpose right – writing to argue, explain, and so on. Prepare yourself for this by taking a topic you know well (for example a hobby or knowledge of a singer or band) and writing some sample opening paragraphs for different text types – e.g. a leaflet on the topic, a letter, some instructions.
- Remember the importance of sentence variety. Practise this in advance of the exam so that it becomes a natural part of your writing style.
- Remember that top grade candidates tend to write short sentences as much as long sentences. Aim for variety.
- Remember the importance of accurate spelling and punctuation. Work on learning those spellings that you sometimes struggle with.

GLOSSARY OF ENGLISH AND ENGLISH LITERATURE TERMS

Use this checklist to make sure you understand the key words used during your English and English Literature course.

Active and passive

An active sentence gives the subject first. The passive voice turns a sentence around so that the object comes first and the subject is placed later. An active sentence might be:

The burglar smashed the kitchen window.

The passive voice places emphasis on what happened rather than on who did it:

The kitchen window was smashed by the burglar.

The passive voice will sometimes leave the subject out altogether:

The kitchen window was smashed.

The passive voice is not very common in most speech and writing, except in some types of texts. It can be useful where the speaker/writer wishes to:

◆ withhold information at first
◆ conceal information altogether
◆ build suspense
◆ give emphasis to what happened, rather than who did it.

Adjective   A word which gives more information about a noun or pronoun – e.g. *the **unlucky** team; he is **ugly***.

Adverb   A word which gives more information about a verb – e.g. *The man skipped **childishly***. Adverbs can tell us about manner (*childishly*), time (*yesterday*) and place (*here*).

Agreement   The process by which a verb is altered to match the number and person of its subject: *he thinks* (not *think*); *they think* (not *thinks*).

Alliteration   The term used to describe a series of words next to or near each other, which all begin with the same sound. This creates particular sound effects, e.g. *wet, windy weather*.

Ambiguity   Words, phrases or texts which are open to different interpretations, or language which may be understood in diverse ways. Verbal compression in poetry, book titles and newspaper headlines often leads to ambiguity:

Giant waves down tunnel

Generals fly back to front

Apostrophe   A punctuation mark used for two different purposes.

1   It shows when two words have been compressed into one (*did + not = didn't*). We use this type of expression more in informal situations.
2   It shows that something belongs to someone (*Ted's temper*). The apostrophe can inform the reader about whether the noun is singular (just one) or plural (more than one) according to its position. For example, in *I watched the boy's bad behaviour* the placing of the apostrophe after *boy* shows that there is just one boy. In *I watched the boys' bad behaviour*, the apostrophe is placed after the plural, *boys*, so we know that there is more than one boy.

Association   A word can suggest a range of associations and connections in addition to its straightforward dictionary meaning. For example, *heart* has many associations with love, courage and other human values, besides its literal, biological meaning.

Assonance   The repetition of identical or similar vowel sounds in neighbouring words. It is distinct from rhyme in that the consonants differ while the vowels match.

*Shark, bre**a**thing ben**ea**th the sea,*
*Has no bel**ie**f commits no tre**a**son.*

Auxiliary verb   A verb form used before the main verb to change its meaning – such as to indicate number and tense:

auxiliary verb/s	main verb
is	*studying*
are	*studying*
has been	*studying*
will	*study*
might	*study*

The most common auxiliary verbs are *to be* (*is/was/are/am/were*) and *to have* (*has/had/have*).

Ballad   A ballad is a simple song or poem, which tells a story. Traditional folk ballad form varies, but usually includes these features:

- regular stanzas of four lines each
- lines 2 and 4 have full end-rhymes
- a strong, regular rhythm
- use of simple language – words of one or two syllables
- use of repetition or a refrain
- the use of simple direct speech
- a minimum of description
- impersonal, third-person narrative viewpoint.

Blank verse   Blank verse is unrhymed and echoes the natural rhythm of English speech. Poets such as Shakespeare, Milton, Wordsworth and Tennyson have used it in drama and lyric poetry.

Each line of blank verse has ten syllables – five unstressed and five stressed. Each metrical unit (or foot) has one unstressed and one stressed syllable. A line arranged in this way, with five pairs of unstressed and stressed syllables, is described as **iambic pentameter**.

One equal temper of heroic hearts,
Made weak by time and fate, but strong in will
To strive, to seek, to find and not to yield.
        (Alfred, Lord Tennyson)

Clause   A group of words formed around a verb. They are used to make up sentences. This compound sentence contains two clauses linked by *and*:

The actor left the stage and the audience broke into applause.

The complex sentence below also contains two clauses. One is the **main clause** (it carries the main information). The second is the **subordinate** or **dependent** clause (it gives background detail):

The actor left the stage, carrying his sword before him.

Colon   A punctuation mark which introduces something else, such as a list, quotation, or statement, within the sentence. For example:

Please bring the following: 6 knives, 6 forks, and 12 glasses.

Comma   Commas are used:

- to separate items in a list or strings of adjectives, e.g. *the cool, damp evening was approaching*
- to introduce direct speech and replace the full stop at the end of the spoken sentence, e.g. *He said, 'Hello.' 'Hi,' she replied.*)
- to mark off a relative clause, e.g. *The dog, which had now stopped barking, trotted off along the street*
- to mark off many connecting adverbs, e.g. *Suddenly, she darted into an alleyway*
- to attach a question tag to a statement, e.g. *You do like this, don't you?*
- after a subordinate clause which begins a sentence, e.g. *Because it had started raining, we went indoors.*

Compound   Word formed by joining two words together – e.g. *babysitter, blackbird.*

Conjunction   A word used for joining sentences and ideas together. The most commonly used examples are *and, but, or, because.*

Connective   A word or phrase that helps us to make connections between different ideas in a text. Typical examples include: *on the other hand; however; in fact*. Each of these gives a hint that the sentence or paragraph which follows will connect with what has gone before – giving a different argument (*on the other hand / however*) or adding more information (*in fact*).

Dash   Punctuation mark used to add information, or – sometimes – to bracket off ideas, as in this sentence.

Dialect   A variety of English. Just as there are different varieties of breakfast cereal, some sweet, some healthy, some crunchy, some smooth, so English has variation in vocabulary and grammatical constructions. The word *hedgehog* is used in some regions; *urchin* is preferred in other places. The sentence *I'll teach you that later* is the normal way of speaking in some places; in others you might say *I'll learn you that later*. Dialects remind us of our roots – the way language has developed differently in different regions over hundreds of years. In formal situations and in writing, standard English is usually used.

Direct speech   A speaker's words or thoughts, placed within speech marks.

Dramatic irony   A form of irony in drama in which the audience knows more about a character's situation than the character does, and can foresee consequences that the character cannot. In J.B. Priestley's *An Inspector Calls*, written in 1946 but set in 1912, a character describes the *Titanic* as *'unsinkable, absolutely unsinkable'*.

Emotive language   Language that provokes a strong emotional response.

Enjambment   Where lines of poetry are not stopped at the end, either by sense or punctuation, and run over into the next line. The completion of the phrase, clause or sentence is held over. For example:

A thing of beauty is a joy for ever
Its loveliness increases; it will never
Pass into nothingness; but will keep
A bower quiet for us, and a sleep
Full of sweet dreams, and health, and quiet breathing.
   (John Keats)

Exclamation mark   A punctuation mark used to show urgency or emotion, e.g. *Look out!*

Full stop   A punctuation mark used to mark the ends of sentences.

Genre   A type or category of writing, e.g. science fiction, horror and detective writing are categories of fiction.

Hyperbole   Exaggeration for the sake of emphasis or comic effect, e.g. *I've waited here for ages.*

Hyphen   A punctuation mark used to join two words together (*hat-trick* means something different from *hat trick*). They are also used to show where words have been split at the ends of lines.

Imperative   The form of a verb used to give a command – e.g. *Leave now!*

Infinitive   The form of a verb that lacks a tense and stands for the verb as a whole – e.g. *to eat / we can eat*.

Inflection   The way words change their shape to show, for example, that they are singular or plural (e.g. *table* becomes *tables*) and to indicate tense (e.g. *change* becomes *changes / changed / changing*).

Irony   A relationship of inconsistency or contrast between what is actually said and what is meant. In verbal irony, this takes the form of a discrepancy between the literal meaning of the language used and the inferred meaning. In structural irony, a character is seen to be naïve or mistaken as his or her view of the world is very different from the true circumstances recognized by the author and readers.

Irregular form   Where a word has an unusual inflected form rather than following the regular pattern of inflection (e.g. *brought* not *bringed*, *mice* not *mouses*).

Metaphor   The most widespread figure of speech. In metaphor, one thing is compared to another without using the linking words *like* or *as*, so it is more direct than a simile. One thing is actually said to **be** the other, e.g. *My brother is a pig. His room is a pig sty.*

Verbs can also be used metaphorically: love *blossoms*. Metaphors create new ways of viewing familiar objects and are also commonly found in everyday speech, e.g. *the root of the problem.*

Narrative verse   Poems, including ballads and epics, which tell stories.

Narrative viewpoint   There are two main narrative viewpoints. In a first-person narrative, the narrator is a character in the story who retells his or her first-hand account of events. In a third-person narrative, the narrative voice stands outside the story and is not a character. This type of narrative voice tends to be more objective and often is omniscient (that is, all-seeing) and able to show the reader the thoughts of all the characters.

Noun   A word which labels a person, thing or idea. There are four types of noun:

1   Common noun: *train, pizza, dogs*
2   Proper noun: *Pepsi, China, Becky*
3   Abstract noun: *life, sorrow, winter*
4   Collective noun: **pride** *of lions,* **herd** *of cattle.*

Onomatopoeia   Where words sound like the things they describe, e.g. *buzz, creak, murmur, bang, crash.*

Oxymoron   A figure of speech that combines two contradictory terms, e.g. *bitter sweet, living death, wise fool.*

Paragraph   A group of sentences linked together by their theme or topic. Paragraph breaks are useful in fiction texts to indicate:

◆   a change of speaker
◆   a change of time
◆   a change of place
◆   a change of viewpoint.

In non-fiction texts, new paragraphs are used for:

◆   a change of topic
◆   to make a new point within a topic
◆   a change of time
◆   a change of viewpoint.

Passive voice   *See* Active and passive

Pathetic fallacy   The description of a natural phenomenon, for example the weather or the sea, as if it could feel emotion and is in sympathy with the mood of the poet or the characters.

Pattern of three   A structure used in rhetoric to persuade and make an argument more effective, involving giving three examples:

Never in the field of human conflict was so much owed by so many to so few.
(From a speech by Winston Churchill following the Battle of Britain)

Personification   A form of figurative language in which animals, inanimate objects and abstract ideas are addressed or described as if they were human, e.g. *The breeze whispered gently.*

Phrase   A group of words which makes sense within a clause or sentence but cannot stand on its own — e.g. *the old grey mare; my house; speaking slowly.*

Plural   More than one.

Prefix   Letters added to the beginning of a word to change its meaning (e.g. *un+pleasant*).

Preposition   A word used chiefly to show where something or someone is – for example *in, on, under*. Sometimes we use 'multi-word' prepositions – *ahead of, near to, in addition to*.

Pronoun   A word which can be used in place of a noun – e.g. *The Mayor visited today. Did* **you** *see* **him**?

Pun   A play on words, often for humorous effect, in which two different meanings are suggested either by the same word, or two similar sounding words. Shakespeare uses many puns. In *Romeo and Juliet* the dying Mercutio says, *Ask for me tomorrow and you shall find me a grave man.*

Punctuation   The marks we use in writing (such as commas, full stops and capital letters) to help the reader understand our ideas. They are the written equivalent of the way we use tone of voice and pauses in speech.

Question mark   A punctuation mark used to indicate that the sentence is a question. In speech, we raise the pitch of our voice at the end to show that the sentence is a question.

Refrain   A line repeated at regular or irregular intervals throughout a poem, usually at the end of each stanza.

Register   The way we change our use of language in different situations. We might use a formal register in a school assembly: *Good morning, today I wish to discuss . . .* An informal register might be used with friends: *Hi, I've got something to tell you . . .*

Relative clause   A group of words built around a verb, which can be added to sentences to give more detail. A simple sentence is *My brother has chickenpox.* A relative clause can be added after the subject: *My brother, who was four last week, has chickenpox.*

You can add relative clauses at other points too: *My brother has chickenpox, which is a shame.*

Relative pronoun   A word such as *who, which* and *that*, used at the start of relative clauses.

Rhetorical question   A question asked only in order to emphasize a point of view and to persuade the reader to agree, not as a real request for information – e.g. *Do we really want to encourage young people to smoke?*

Rhyme   Rhyme is often used in poetry to create patterns of similar sounds. Words are said to rhyme when their end sounds match, or sound the same.

There are many different types of rhyme. Below are definitions for some of these:

End rhyme
When the last word in a line of poetry rhymes with the last word in another line.

Internal rhyme
When a word in the middle of a line rhymes with a word at the end of the line.

Full rhyme
When two words rhyme completely, e.g. *cry* and *dry*; *heaven* and *Devon*.

Sight rhyme
Where two words look from their spelling as if they should rhyme, but in fact the sounds of the words do not rhyme – e.g. *love* and *move; cost* and *post*.

Rhyming couplet
A rhyme scheme where one line of poetry rhymes with the following line, e.g.

And moveless fish in the water gleam
By silver reeds in a silver stream.

Rhyme scheme   The pattern in which rhyming lines occur in a poem is called its rhyme scheme. To describe a poem's rhyme scheme, letters of the alphabet are often used to show which lines rhyme with which others. Each different rhyming word is given a different letter:

I wander'd lonely as a cloud (a)
That floats on high o'er vales and hills (b)
When all at once I saw a crowd (a)
A host of golden daffodils (b)
Beside the lake, beneath the trees (c)
Fluttering and dancing in the breeze. (c)

In the above stanza from William Wordsworth's famous poem 'The Daffodils', the rhyme scheme is *ababcc* – line 1 rhymes with line 3; line 2 rhymes with line 4 and lines 5 and 6 rhyme. Lines 5 and 6 form a rhyming couplet.

Rhythm A major difference between poetry and prose is that poems often have a more regular or obvious rhythm. The term 'rhythm' is used to refer to the pattern of beats created by the words in a poem and the way they are organized. Some words or syllables are emphasized more than others. For example, in the three-syllable word *secretary*, we emphasize (or stress) the first syllable more than the others.

Root words Words which can have prefixes and suffixes added to them in order to change their meanings, e.g. *pleasant* becomes *unpleasant*; *happy* becomes *happiness*.

Semi-colon A punctuation mark that indicates a break which is not as strong as a full stop but stronger than a comma. It often replaces the word *and* between clauses and phrases on a similar topic, or separates longer items in a list.

Sentence A group of words which can stand on their own. We expect sentences to:

- contain a main verb
- begin with a capital letter
- end with a full stop, question mark or exclamation mark.

Sentence functions The purposes of sentences: they can be statements, questions, commands and exclamations.

Sentence types Simple, compound, and complex. A **simple** sentence contains a single subject, a single verb or verb phrase, and makes sense on its own:

The big black cat is chasing a little mouse.

Sentences can be joined together using the conjunctions *and, or* or *but*. This makes simple sentences into **compound** (or **co-ordinated**) sentences. For example, two simple sentences . . .

Text messaging can be fun. It keeps you in touch with friends.

. . . can become one compound sentence:

Text messaging can be fun and it keeps you in touch with friends.

Complex sentences are created by using conjunctions between clauses, or at the start of sentences, such as *until, although, before, since, because:*

He kept running although his knee hurt.

Because his pursuers had disappeared, he stopped running.

The relative pronouns *who, which,* or *that* can also be used to add information and create a complex sentence:

The men who were chasing him had taken another track.

Sibilance The recurrence of sounds known as sibilants, which 'hiss' (*s, sh, zh, c, ch*):

Ships that pass in the night, and speak each other in passing;
Only a signal shown and a distant voice in the darkness.
   (Henry Longfellow)

Simile In a simile, one thing is compared to another using the linking words *like* or *as*, e.g. *My brother eats like a pig and his room is as messy as a pig-sty.*

Singular   A word applied to nouns to show that there is only one of them – e.g. *desk, computer, telephone*. These are all singular. To become plural, each would gain an *-s*. Some words are the same in their singular and plural forms – e.g. *one sheep; 20 sheep*.

Soliloquy   In drama, the convention by which a character speaks his or her thoughts aloud, alone on the stage. The best-known example of a soliloquy is Hamlet's 'To be or not to be' speech.

Sonnet   A sonnet is a short, lyric poem with 14 rhyming lines of equal length. Each line has ten syllables, made up of five pairs of unstressed and stressed syllables. This is known as **iambic pentameter**.

Standard English   The most important dialect or variety of English. It is used in most written texts, in education, in law, and in the media. It is the form of English defined in dictionaries.

Subject and object   The subject is the person or thing in a sentence that is doing the action of the verb. In *Mary shouted at Kim*, Mary is the subject – she is doing the shouting. The object is the person who receives the action – in this case, Kim.

Suffix   Letters added to the end of a word to change its meaning – e.g. *tact + less*.

Synonym   A word which has a similar meaning to another word. Synonyms for *fire* include: *blaze, flames, inferno, conflagration*. You would choose different words according to the register you were using.

Tense   English changes the ending of verbs to show the present and past tenses: She *walk+s* . . . she *walk+ed*.

To show the future tense, we sometimes use the present tense verb with an adverbial:

The plane leaves soon
The plane leaves in five minutes
The plane leaves tomorrow

We can also create the future tense by using modal verbs – *will / would / shall / might*:

*The plane **will** leave in five minutes*
*The plane **might** leave in five minutes*

Topic sentence   A sentence at the start of a text or paragraph which tells you what the content will be. Newspaper stories usually start with topic sentences: they tell you *who, where,* and *when.* For example:

A 77-year old man was dramatically rescued in Leicester last night when flames threatened to engulf his house.

Verb   A word which tells us what someone or something is doing – e.g. *She **saw** the fox. It **ran** across the road.*

Verb chain or verb phrase   Sometimes we use a number of verbs together to add detail, for example about tense (when something happened). For example:

I eat – main verb
I have eaten – verb chain (*have* = auxiliary verb, *eaten* = main verb)
I will eat – verb chain (*will* = auxiliary verb, *eat* = main verb)
I would have eaten – verb chain (*would* = auxiliary verb, *have* = auxiliary verb, *eaten* = main verb)

Word class   A group of words with a particular function in a sentence – nouns, verbs, adjectives, adverbs, prepositions, conjunctions, and so on.

GLOSSARY OF EXAM TERMS

Success in examinations depends not only on knowledge but also on the ability to turn facts into examination marks. The first step in doing this is to make sure that you **follow the instructions given in a question**. You won't gain marks unless you do what the examiner wants you to do!

The examiners want to be as helpful as possible (really, they do!) and so they think very carefully about the instructions that they use in their questions. The list below contains some of the most common instructions used in English examinations, and explains what these instructions mean.

INSTRUCTION	WHAT DOES THE EXAMINER WANT YOU TO DO?
Imagine	Put yourself into a situation and write about it. You might be asked to 'imagine you have bought a product that has gone wrong. Write a letter to complain . . .' The secret here is to think what it must be like to be in that situation. You might be asked to imagine you are a character in a story or other text. Again, the secret is to look through that character's eyes. In practical terms, remember to: ◆ write in the first person 'I . . . me' ◆ get the style right – formal for a letter of complaint; informal for a diary entry ◆ use vocabulary which is appropriate – interesting and lively without being too flashy
Inform	Tell the reader about something. You might be asked to communicate new information in a different format – e.g. write a leaflet on healthy eating. You might need to take details from a text and present them in a way that is easy to understand. The secret is to know your audience. Write as clearly as possible so that the reader understands what you are saying.
Describe	Show how something works. You might be asked to show how a writer builds tension in a text, or to write in detail about an experience that has happened to you. The secret is detail. 'Describe' requires close attention to details, whether in a text, or from your own experience.
Persuade	Make the reader think something different. Persuasive texts try to change our beliefs and opinions. You might be asked to write a letter persuading people to give support to a charity. You might be asked to create an advertisement, leaflet or poster. The secret is to use language and layout so that your reader believes your ideas and attitudes, or believes in the product you are promoting.
Explain	Show how something works. You might show how a writer gives us hints about a character, or show that you understand the meanings of words in a text. 'Explain' requires clarity. You need to be able to show your own understanding, and communicate your ideas clearly and precisely to your audience.